Independent Task Force Report No. 77

Innovation and National Security

Keeping Our Edge

James Manyika and William H. McRaven, *Chairs*
Adam Segal, *Project Director*

TASK FORCE MEMBERS

Task Force members are asked to join a consensus signifying that they endorse "the general policy thrust and judgments reached by the group, though not necessarily every finding and recommendation." They participate in the Task Force in their individual, not their institutional, capacities.

Alana Ackerson★
Figure

Doug Beck
Apple

Nicholas F. Beim
Venrock

Jim Breyer
Breyer Capital

Steven A. Denning★
General Atlantic

Regina E. Dugan
Independent Consultant

Reid Hoffman
Greylock Partners

Amir Husain
SparkCognition

Nicole Y. Lamb-Hale
Kroll, a Division of Duff & Phelps

Eric S. Lander
Broad Institute

James Manyika
McKinsey & Company

William H. McRaven
Lyndon B. Johnson School of Public Affairs, University of Texas, Austin

Mira Patel
Facebook

DJ Patil★
Devoted Health

L. Rafael Reif
Massachusetts Institute of Technology

Eric Schmidt
Alphabet

Adam Segal
Council on Foreign Relations

Raj M. Shah★
Arceo.ai

Laura D'Andrea Tyson★
Haas School of Business, University of California, Berkeley

Jerry Yang★
AME Cloud Ventures

CONTENTS

FOREWORD

For the past three-quarters of a century, the United States has led the world in technological innovation and development. Catalyzed by the Sputnik satellite launch and the need to compete with the Soviet Union, the United States invested heavily in scientific research and development (R&D). Technologies integral to our daily lives, including the internet, Global Positioning System (GPS), touch screens, solar panels, and LED technology, are in part or in whole the result of research sponsored by U.S. federal agencies. These investments helped propel the United States to become the richest nation on earth and ensure that its military enjoyed a qualitative edge over rivals'.

Today, however, the United States risks falling behind its competitors, principally China. U.S. federal R&D as a percentage of gross domestic product (GDP) peaked at above 2 percent in the 1970s and has declined since, from a little over 1 percent in 2001 to 0.7 percent in 2018. In 2015, for the first time since World War II, the federal government provided less than half of all funding for basic research. China, meanwhile, is catching up, having increased its R&D expenditures by an average of 18 percent annually since 2000. Indeed, the Task Force concludes that China is closing the gap with the United States and will soon be one of the leading powers in emerging technologies.

In addition to the challenge posed by China, the accelerating pace of innovation, which is increasingly disruptive and transformative to societies, makes finding policy responses more difficult. Many advanced technologies necessary for national security are developed in the private sector and built via complex supply chains that span the globe, making it harder for the U.S. government to use traditional policy levers to shape the manufacturing base. Further, the strained relationship between the Department of Defense and elements of the private sector means that adopting new technologies to strengthen national security can be tough.

The Task Force argues the United States needs to respond urgently and comprehensively over the next five years and put forward a national security innovation strategy to ensure it is the predominant power in a range of emerging technologies such as AI and data science, advanced battery storage, advanced semiconductor technologies, genomics and synthetic biology, fifth-generation cellular networks (5G), quantum information systems, and robotics.

Such a strategy, the Task Force concludes, should be based on four pillars: restoring federal funding for R&D, attracting and educating a science and technology workforce, supporting technology adoption in the defense sector, and bolstering and scaling technology alliances. Given that many new technologies now used in the military sphere are first developed in the civilian sector, public-private partnerships will be needed. The Task Force report puts forward an array of thoughtful policy prescriptions for the federal government, industry, and academia to achieve the goal of maintaining U.S. leadership.

In concrete terms, federal support for basic R&D will need to increase. Although private-sector investment has risen over the past three decades, it is no substitute for federally funded R&D that targets national strategic concerns. The report argues that "only the government can make the type of investments in basic science that ignite discoveries; such investments are too big and risky for any single private enterprise to undertake."

The Task Force recommends the United States introduce additional scholarships and modify immigration policies to enable its world-class universities to attract and educate a science and technology workforce.

U.S. federal agencies and military services should also devote a greater share of their budgets to supporting technology integration and reform their institutional cultures to allow for better integration of new technologies.

The United States should partner with like-minded countries to develop common policies for the use and control of emerging technologies and work with major trading partners to promote the free flow of data and development of common technology standards. In this context, Washington's current trade policies needlessly alienate partners, raise costs for American tech firms, and impede the adoption of U.S. technology in foreign markets, and thus will harm U.S. innovative capabilities.

If it succeeds, the United States will continue to enjoy economic, strategic, and military advantages over potential rivals and would-be challengers. Failure, the Task Force rightly concludes, will lead to a future in which "rivals strengthen their militaries and threaten U.S. security interests, and new innovation centers replace the United States as the source of original ideas and inspiration for the world."

An additional word on China. The Task Force finds that China wants to dominate the industries of the future and in a decade will likely spend more than any other country on R&D. While the Task Force "commends the White House for confronting China on cyber espionage and IP [intellectual property] theft," it also finds that "the administration is over-weaponizing trade policy, with long-term costs to U.S. innovation capabilities." The Task Force concludes, "Slowing China down is not as effective as outpacing it." The best way to answer China's challenge is to compete more effectively. The response to this challenge must truly begin at home.

I would like to thank the Task Force chairs, James Manyika and William H. McRaven, for their significant contribution to this important project. My thanks extend to all the Task Force members for similarly lending their knowledge and experience. This report would not have been possible without CFR's Adam Segal, who directed the Task Force and authored this report, and CFR's Independent Task Force Program Director Anya Schmemann, who ably guided this project. They too have earned our thanks for taking on so complex and critical a subject.

Richard N. Haass
President
Council on Foreign Relations
September 2019

ACKNOWLEDGMENTS

The report of the Independent Task Force on U.S. Innovation Strategy and National Security is the product of its members, who graciously shared their time and expertise with us. I am grateful for the input and feedback they provided throughout this project. In particular, I would like to thank our co-chairs, James Manyika and Bill McRaven, for their strong vision and thoughtful leadership; it was a genuine pleasure to work with them.

All the Task Force members contributed, but special thanks go to Task Force members Nick Beim and Regina Dugan, who were extremely generous with their time and energy, providing input and advice on all the drafts as well as some significant cheerleading as the report neared completion. Task Force members Doug Beck, Reid Hoffman, Amir Husain, Nicole Lamb-Hale, DJ Patil, Raj Shah, and Laura Tyson also sent useful comments, edits, and recommendations to me, while others shared helpful thoughts with our co-chairs.

I am also thankful to several individuals and organizations who provided input and assistance over the course of our project, including: Michael Brown and Pavneet Singh, Defense Innovation Unit; Pat Gelsinger, VMware; Michael McNerney, Arbor Networks; Sean Randolph, Bay Area Council; Dave Rey, Peter Schwartz, and Fred Tsai, Salesforce; Martin A. Schmidt, Massachusetts Institute of Technology (MIT); and Kent Walker, Google. I am especially grateful to David Goldston, MIT, for his comments and close readings of the report drafts. Thanks go to Michael Kratsios, deputy assistant to the president for technology policy and deputy U.S. chief technology officer, and Andrew Ng, founder and CEO of Landing AI, who provided expert briefings to the Task Force group. I am also grateful to National Intelligence Council experts Michael Allison, Greg Hebner, Kurt

Miller, Anna Puglisi, and Anthony Schinella for meeting with us, and to Defense Innovation Board Executive Director Joshua Marcuse and board members Michael McQuade, Milo Medin, Richard Murray, and Mark Sirangelo for convening a teleconference to exchange ideas. Our thanks to McKinsey & Company and Sarah Portik for hosting a Task Force meeting in San Francisco.

Further, I appreciate the contributions from CFR's members who attended events related to this Task Force, including roundtables in Boston, New York, Palo Alto, San Francisco, and Washington. Thanks to CFR's Corporate, Meetings, and National Programs for arranging these sessions, and to those Task Force members who lent their time to serve as presiders or panelists for these and other events.

My gratitude extends to all those at CFR who made this report possible. Several research associates and interns contributed to this report: I am grateful to Lorand Laskai for his early, superb research support; Kanzanira Thorington for her contributions to the data and graphics; Benjamin Della Rocca for his assistance with data; and Lauren Dudley for her help getting the report across the finish line. CFR's Publications team deserves recognition for ably preparing the report for publication, and CFR's Digital team did great work designing the report and producing the graphics that appear throughout the text. Independent Task Force Program Director Anya Schmemann managed the smooth execution of this project from start to finish, and I am grateful to her and her teammates Chelie Setzer and Sara Shah for their support in convening meetings, editing drafts, and planning for the report's outreach. Finally, I am thankful to CFR President Richard N. Haass for his vision and for providing this opportunity.

While this report is the product of the Independent Task Force, the responsibility for any omissions or errors is mine. Once again, my sincere thanks to all who contributed.

Adam Segal
Project Director

INDEPENDENT
TASK FORCE REPORT

EXECUTIVE SUMMARY

The United States leads the world in innovation, research, and technology development. Since World War II, the new markets, industries, companies, and military capabilities that emerged from the country's science and technology commitment have combined to make the United States the most secure and economically prosperous nation on earth. This seventy-year strength arose from the expansion of economic opportunities at home through substantial investments in education and infrastructure, unmatched innovation and talent ecosystems, and the opportunities and competition created by the opening of new markets and the global expansion of trade. It was also forged in the fire of threat: It was formed and tested in military conflicts from the Cold War to the war in Afghanistan, in technological leadership lost and regained during competition with Japan in the 1980s, and in the internal cultural conflicts over the role of scientists in aiding the Pentagon during the Vietnam War. Confronted with a threat to national security or economic competitiveness, the United States responded. So must it once again.

This time there is no Sputnik satellite circling the earth to catalyze a response, but the United States faces a convergence of forces that equally threaten its economic and national security. First, the pace of innovation globally has accelerated, and it is more disruptive and transformative to industries, economies, and societies. Second, many advanced technologies necessary for national security are developed in the private sector by firms that design and build them via complex supply chains that span the globe; these technologies are then deployed in global markets. The capacities and vulnerabilities of the manufacturing base are far more complex than in previous eras, and the ability of the U.S. Department of Defense (DOD) to control manufacturing-base activity using traditional policy means has been greatly reduced. Third, China, now the world's second-largest economy, is both a U.S. economic partner and a strategic competitor, and it constitutes a different type of challenger.[1] Tightly interconnected with the United States, China is launching government-led investments, increasing its numbers of science and engineering graduates, and mobilizing large pools of data and global technology companies in pursuit of ambitious economic and strategic goals.

The United States has had a time-tested playbook for technological competition. It invests in basic research and development (R&D), making discoveries that radically change understanding of existing scientific concepts and serve as springs for later-stage development activities in private industry and government. It trains and nurtures science, technology, engineering, and mathematics (STEM) talent at home, and it attracts and retains the world's best students and practitioners. It wins new markets abroad and links emerging technology ecosystems to domestic innovations through trade relationships and alliances. And it converts new technological advances into military capabilities faster than its potential adversaries.

Erosion in the country's leadership in any of these steps that drive and diffuse technological advances would warrant a powerful reply. However, the United States faces a critical inflection point in all of them. There is a great deal of talk among policymakers, especially in the Defense Department, about the importance of innovation, but the rhetoric does not translate fast enough into changes that matter. The Task Force believes that the government and the private sector must undertake a comprehensive and urgent response to this challenge over the next five years. Failure to do so will mean a future in which other countries reap the lion's share of the benefits of technological development, rivals strengthen their militaries and threaten U.S. security interests, and new innovation centers replace the United States as the source of original ideas and inspiration for the world.

The major findings of the Task Force are:

- Countries that can harness the current wave of innovation, mitigate its potential disruptions, and capitalize on its transformative power will gain economic and military advantages over potential rivals.

- The United States has led the world in innovation, research, and technology development since World War II, but that leadership is now at risk.

- U.S. leadership in science and technology is at risk because of a decades-long stagnation in federal support and funding for research and development. Private-sector investment has risen, but it is not a substitute for federally funded R&D directed at national economic, strategic, and social concerns.

- Friends, allies, and collaborators tightly link technology ecosystems and create scale in a globalized system of innovation, and thus are a competitive advantage. Washington's current trade policies needlessly alienate partners, raise costs for American tech firms, and impede the adoption of U.S. technology in foreign markets.

- A central strength of the U.S. innovation environment has been a steady pipeline of domestic STEM talent and the country's ability to attract the best and brightest students, engineers, and scientists from around the world. A lack of strong education initiatives at home and new barriers to talented foreign students' and workers' coming to and remaining in the United States will have long-term negative economic and national security consequences.

- The Defense Department and the intelligence community will fall behind potential adversaries if they do not rapidly access and deploy technologies developed in the private sector.

- The defense community faces severe challenges in attracting and retaining tech talent.

- The defense community faces deteriorating manufacturing capabilities, insecure supply chains, and dependence on competitor nations for hardware.

- A persistent cultural divide between the technology and policymaking communities threatens national security by making it more difficult for the Defense Department and intelligence community to acquire and adopt advanced technologies from the private sector and to draw on technical talent.

- China is investing significant resources in developing new technologies, and after 2030 it will likely be the world's largest spender on research and development. Although Beijing's efforts to become a scientific power could help drive global growth and prosperity, and both the United States and China have benefited from bilateral investment and trade, Chinese theft of intellectual property (IP) and its market-manipulating industrial policies threaten U.S. economic competitiveness and national security.

- China is closing the technological gap with the United States, and though it may not match U.S. capabilities across the board, it will soon be one of the leading powers in technologies such as artificial intelligence (AI), robotics, energy storage, fifth-generation cellular networks (5G), quantum information systems, and possibly biotechnology.

- Although the Donald J. Trump administration has boosted the budgets of several technology-related organizations within the DOD and issued a number of executive orders, its efforts to accelerate innovation in critical frontier technologies such as AI are too incremental and narrow in scale.

- The United States is ahead of the rest of world in AI, but others are closing the gap—and U.S. failure to compete for global talent could result in the loss of its lead.

- In the race for the next generation of communications technologies, the Trump administration has developed only a few parts of what should be a multifaceted strategy. It has failed to coordinate a response to Huawei's global expansion, muddied its message about the company's economic and national security risks, and not sufficiently accelerated domestic efforts to deploy 5G.

- Beijing has often exploited the openness of the American system. Efforts to protect U.S. intellectual property are a necessary complement to, but not a substitute for, innovating faster than China. The administration is over-weaponizing trade and investment policy, with costs to U.S. innovation.

The United States needs a national security innovation strategy that ensures it is the predominant power in a range of emerging and foundational technologies over the next two decades. This Task Force report offers policy recommendations for the federal government, industry, and academia. Progress on this issue will require contributions and creativity from all three sectors if the United States is to maintain its ability to lead the world in the scientific and technological innovations necessary to its security and economic vitality. Some of the recommendations can be implemented in the short term; others will require more systemic change.

A new U.S. innovation strategy should be based on four pillars: funding, talent, technology adoption, and technology alliances and ecosystems. Action is required over the next five years. The major recommendations of the Task Force are:

Restore Federal Funding for Research and Development

- The White House and Congress should restore federal funding for research and development to its historical average. This would mean increasing funding from 0.7 percent to 1.1 percent of gross domestic product (GDP) annually, or from $146 billion to about $230 billion (in 2018 dollars). Only the government can make the type of investments in basic science that ignite discoveries; such investments are too big and risky for any single private enterprise to undertake.

- Federal and state governments should make an additional strategic investment in universities. The investment, of up to $20 billion a year for five years, should support cross-disciplinary work in areas of pressing economic and national security interest.

- The White House should announce moonshot approaches to society-wide national security problems. This would support innovation in foundational and general-purpose technologies, including AI and data science, advanced battery storage, advanced semiconductors, genomics and synthetic biology, 5G, quantum information systems, and robotics.

Attract and Educate a Science and Technology Workforce

- The White House, Congress, and academia should develop a twenty-first-century National Defense Education Act (NDEA), with the goal of expanding the pipeline of talent in science, technology, engineering, and mathematics. A twenty-first-century NDEA would support up to twenty-five thousand competitive STEM undergraduate scholarships and five thousand graduate fellowships.

- Universities, federal and state government, and business should address the underrepresentation of minorities and women in STEM fields through mentoring, training, research experience, and academic and career advising. They should also provide financial support for room and board, tuition and fees, and books, as well as assessments of job placement opportunities in STEM fields, highlighting employers with clear track records of fairness in hiring, promotion, and pay.

- Federal agencies, the private sector, and universities should work together to support debt forgiveness for students going into specialized technology sectors.

- The United States needs to make it easier for foreign graduates of U.S. universities in scientific and technical fields to remain and work in the country. Congress should "staple a green card to an advanced diploma," granting lawful permanent residence to those who earn a STEM master's degree or doctorate. Congress should also pass the Development, Relief, and Education for Alien Minors (DREAM) Act.

- Congress should pass legislation that permits immigrants to live and work in the United States if they can raise funds to start new companies.

- The federal government should make targeted—rather than sweeping—efforts to prevent the theft of scientific knowledge from American universities.

Support Technology Adoption in the Defense Sector

- Federal agencies and each of the military services should dedicate between 0.5 and 1 percent of their budgets to the rapid integration of technology. The heads of each agency should also hire a domain specialist deputy for fast-track technologies (for example, data sciences, robotics, and genomics) from outside the government for a two- to four-year assignment.

- Congress should establish a new service academy, the U.S. Digital Service Academy, and a Reserve Officer Training Corps for advanced technologies (ROTC-T) to foster the next generation of tech talent.

- Lifelong career paths should be complemented with more short-term, flexible options. The White House and Congress should bring people from the technology industry into all three branches of the government for temporary rotations. They should also develop new fellowships to encourage the circulation of technologists, military officers, and federal officials between the technology sector and the Defense Department.

Bolster and Scale Technology Alliances and Ecosystems

- The State and Treasury Departments should create a technology alliance to develop common policies for the use and control of emerging technologies.

- The Department of Commerce should work with major trading partners to promote the secure and free flow of data and the development of common technology standards.

- The Department of Commerce and the U.S. International Development Finance Corporation should encourage American start-ups in AI and data science, genomics and synthetic biology, quantum information systems, and other frontier technologies to invest in, export to, and form R&D partnerships with firms in emerging technology ecosystems. The goal would be fostering early adopters, developers, and customers who will build on U.S. technologies.

- The Department of Energy (DOE), Department of State, National Institutes of Health (NIH), National Science Foundation (NSF), Office of Science and Technology Policy (OSTP), and other relevant agencies should develop a network of international cooperative science and technology partnerships, open to governments and the private sector, to apply frontier technologies to shared global challenges, such as climate change. Federal agencies should not only fund efforts that will include cooperation with other nations' science organizations but should also provide R&D and tax incentives for tech firms to form international collaborative partnerships.

During the early years of the Cold War, confronted by serious technological and military competition from the Soviet Union, the United States invested heavily in its scientific base. Those investments ensured U.S. technological leadership for fifty years. Faced with the rise of China and a new wave of disruptive technological innovation, the country needs a similar vision and an agenda for realizing it. The United States must once again make technological preeminence a national goal.

INTRODUCTION

Since World War II, U.S. scientific innovation and technological entrepreneurship have ensured the country's economic success and national security. For most of this period, the United States enjoyed global leadership in innovation, measured in research and development spending as well as in patents, scientific paper production, and output from the technology industry. An extraordinary pool of technical and scientific talent generated numerous breakthroughs in economically and strategically important fields. GDP growth in the postwar period depended, in roughly equal measure, on labor supply and productivity growth driven by technological innovation.[2] The United States was the world's largest, most dynamic market, to which other countries and innovators looked for inspiration. Technological predominance supported military leadership, which in turn ushered in a season of unparalleled prosperity.

Today, this leadership position is at risk. The federal government makes investments in basic science that are too big and risky for the private sector to undertake, and these investments can spark discoveries. But over the last two decades, Washington has failed to maintain adequate levels of public support and funding for basic science. Federal investment in R&D as a percentage of GDP peaked at 1.86 percent in 1964 but has declined from a little over 1 percent in 1990 to 0.66 percent in 2016. Current trade policies needlessly alienate friends and allies, increase costs and unpredictability for American tech firms, and impede the adoption of U.S. technology in foreign markets, therefore threatening U.S. science and technology capabilities. The White House is raising new barriers to entry of foreign students and entrepreneurs, undermining the United States' ability to attract and retain global talent. In addition, the Defense Department's acquisition and development processes, designed for stability and predictability, struggle to keep pace with rapid developments in software, physical, and biological systems.

The United States has faced and responded to technological competition in the past. This time, however, developing a national response will be more difficult because of three challenges. First, the pace of innovation has accelerated, with new technologies diffusing to users and businesses much more quickly than they used to. Moreover, new technologies, particularly artificial intelligence, could redefine the nature and role of work, reshaping the economy and challenging local, national, and global political institutions and governance frameworks.

Second, many advanced technologies necessary for national security are multiple-use and developed in the private sector by firms that design and build them via complex supply chains that span the globe. The Defense Department's access to the private sector and new technologies is essential to national security, but the United States has less ability to shape the manufacturing base through traditional policy levers. This private-sector dominance has also resulted in critical technologies' becoming widely available to all countries, even potential adversaries. Military advantages will go to the countries that integrate commercial technologies more quickly.

Third, China is a different type of challenger (see figure 1). The Chinese economy is likely to become larger than the U.S. economy between 2030 and 2040. But the size of the economy may not matter as much as Beijing's promotion of a new model of innovation that combines strategic planning; government-led investments and spending; a permissive regulatory environment; internationally competitive technology platforms; large pools of personal, health, industrial, and other data; and

Figure 1. TOTAL R&D EXPENDITURE BY COUNTRY

Current U.S. dollars

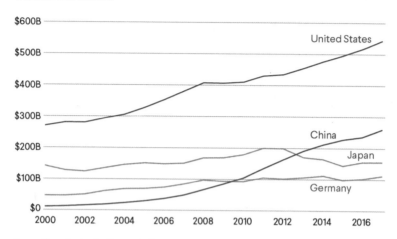

Source: Organization for Economic Cooperation and Development.

growing numbers of skilled STEM talent. Both the U.S. and Chinese science and technology systems have benefited from the countries' close ties and the flow between them of people, money, and products, but China has also taken advantage of the openness of the U.S. innovation system by engaging in the theft of American intellectual property.[3] In addition, the Chinese government is devoting significant resources to converting new science and technology capabilities into military strength.

The United States needs a national security innovation strategy that ensures it is the predominant power over the next two decades in a range of emerging technologies, in particular AI and data science, advanced battery storage, advanced semiconductor technologies, 5G, quantum information systems, and robotics, as well as in critical biotechnologies, including genomics and synthetic biology. Failure to take on these challenges risks the United States' losing the economic and national security benefits it has enjoyed over its decades of technological leadership and investment.

FINDINGS
Speed, Disruption, and Scale

> Countries that can harness the current wave of innovation, mitigate its potential disruptions, and capitalize on its transformative power will gain economic and military advantages over potential rivals.

A new wave of innovation is being driven by the convergence of advances in software, physical, and biological systems.[4] Increased automation, pervasive connectivity, and improved analytics are remaking services and manufacturing. New technologies such as genomics (comprehensive methods for studying the molecular biology of genes, cells, and physiology), additive printing (also known as three-dimensional, or 3-D, printing), and the Internet of Things are merging the physical, biological, and digital worlds.

This wave of innovation is characterized by speed, disruption, and scale. The period between technological breakthroughs is decreasing, and the pace of adoption of technologies is much faster than in the past (see figure 2). After Alexander Graham Bell invented the phone, fifty years passed before half of all American homes had one; but only five years after the invention of the smartphone, half of all Americans had one.[5] It took hundreds of millions of dollars for scientists to sequence the first human genome, in 2004; fifteen years later, machines can sequence genomes for approximately $600 each.[6]

The disruption of technology incumbents is also accelerating. In 1958, companies spent an average of sixty-one years on the S&P 500. By 2011, the average had dropped to seventeen years, and at the current rate

Figure 2. THE PACE OF TECHNOLOGY ADOPTION IS ACCELERATING

Percentage of U.S. households using different technologies

- Landline
- Electric power
- Automobile
- Radio
- Refrigerator
- Color TV
- Microwave
- Computer
- Social media
- Ebook reader
- Tablet

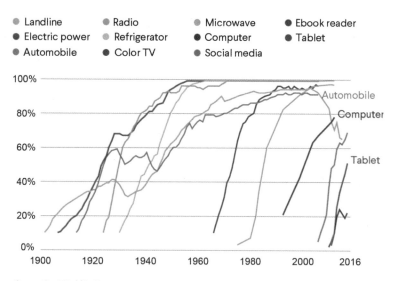

Source: Our World in Data.

of change, in another ten years 75 percent of companies currently on the S&P 500 will be off it. Greater agility is required to remain competitive.

The scope of change is also broader. AI and automation will cause major changes in the workforce, as a previous CFR Independent Task Force report explored.[7] There is a great deal of uncertainty about how much job loss will result: a study from the University of Oxford predicted that 47 percent of U.S. jobs could be automated within the next decade, a McKinsey Global Institute report estimated that 23 percent of jobs could be displaced by automation by 2030, and the Organization for Economic Cooperation and Development (OECD) found that just 9 percent of jobs in the United States were at high risk. But these are gross losses, not net losses, and new jobs are likely to be created by the application of new technology. Therefore, technological change will create losers and winners. Automation tends to complement the expertise, judgment, and creativity of highly educated individuals performing technical, professional, and managerial work. It tends to displace middle-skill (often non-college-educated) workers performing routine tasks that can be coded in production, clerical, administrative, and sales roles. Even with training and educational investments, more Americans may end up working in lower-wage jobs.[8]

These overlapping characteristics make forging a successful innovation strategy more difficult and heighten the costs of failure. Nations that fall behind are likely to lack critical building blocks of economic and military power. They are less likely to have a say in how new technologies are developed and governed around the world.

The U.S. Innovation System

The United States has led the world in innovation, research, and technology development since World War II, but that leadership is now at risk.

Before the war, federal funding for research and development was small. During the war, funding for research and development grew by a factor of twenty, large federal laboratories were founded, and federal money went to universities for research and training. As a result, scientists and engineers made contributions to the war effort, including synthetic rubber, radar, the radio proximity fuse, guided missiles, and the atomic bomb.

Fearing the loss of these efforts after the war, Vannevar Bush, the director of the Office of Scientific Research and Development and the first scientific advisor to a president, delivered a report in 1945 titled *Science: The Endless Frontier* that justified continued federal support for science and technology as the basis of economic and national security. According to Bush, pushing these "new frontiers of the mind" was essential "to our security as a nation, to our better health, to more jobs, to a higher standard of living, and to our cultural progress."[9]

Bush helped formalize a "pipeline" model of radical innovation, focused on creating new-to-the-world products. The innovation process starts with federal investment in R&D, which then passes through universities that promote research and training, and ends with new products that are developed and commercialized in the private sector. Although *Science: The Endless Frontier* laid out a linear model starting with basic research, the reality has always been more complex, with feedback loops between the different stages.

The flow of technologies through the pipeline was often accelerated by the need to respond to political crises.[10] For example, following the Soviet Union's launch of Sputnik in 1957, the Dwight D. Eisenhower administration broadened the front of the pipeline through the National Defense Education Act, which created new graduate fellowships in science and math, provided low-interest loans to undergraduate and graduate students, supported the development of modern curricula in science and math for K–12 education, and funded training institutes for science teachers. Between 1957 and 1961, federal investment in R&D nearly doubled, and total government outlays for basic science at the National Science Foundation and other agencies almost tripled.[11] Congress also supported accelerants at later stages in the pipeline, establishing NASA and the Advanced Research Projects Agency (which became the Defense Advanced Research Projects Agency, or DARPA) to focus on high-risk, high-gain applied development.

Federally supported R&D had a dramatic impact on U.S. competitiveness and national security. According to a 2019 study, starting in the 2010s nearly one-third of patented U.S. inventions relied on federally funded science (see figure 3).[12] Touch screens, the Global Positioning System (GPS), and internet technologies central to the smartphone are all products of Defense Department research. Department of Energy research grants played a role in the development of Tesla's batteries and solar panels, shale gas hydraulic fracturing, light-emitting diode (LED) technology, and 4-D and 5-D seismic imaging. Grants from the NSF were important to the building of the internet, Google's search engine, and magnetic resonance imaging (MRI) machines. Funding

Figure 3. FEDERALLY FUNDED INNOVATIONS

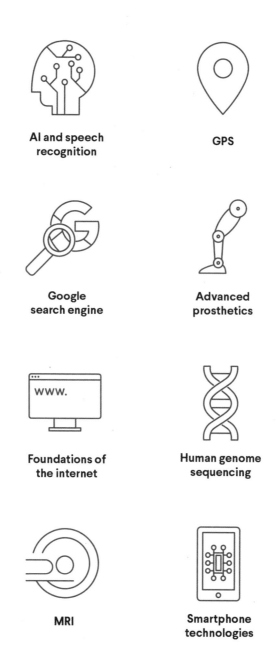

AI and speech
recognition

GPS

Google
search engine

Advanced
prosthetics

Foundations of
the internet

Human genome
sequencing

MRI

Smartphone
technologies

Source: Information Technology and Innovation Foundation.

from the NIH drove research that supported the sequencing of the human genome, advances in prosthetics, and the cancer drug Gleevec (imatinib).[13] Between 1988 and 2010, $3.8 billion of federal investment in genomic research generated an economic impact of $796 billion and created 310,000 jobs.[14] A new wave of support for basic research could have similar economic and military benefits.

The strengths of the U.S. innovation system have been magnified by the U.S. role as a central node in a global network of research and development. Multilateral trade agreements promoted the (relatively) free flow of goods, investment, and—more recently—services and data. Federal agencies pursued a wide range of international cooperative projects on clean energy, pandemic response, food security, and other transnational challenges. U.S. companies opened R&D centers and developed research partnerships in places such as Beijing, China; Bengaluru, India; Dublin, Ireland; Haifa, Israel; Manchester, United Kingdom; and Toronto, Canada. American universities have long had large foreign student populations and partnerships with their foreign peers, and U.S. scientists were the coauthors of choice on scientific papers at higher rates than their counterparts abroad. Innovation was driven in part by the inclusive institutions and networks that connected the United States to the rest of the world.

The United States' open, democratic system was a beacon for talented scientists and engineers from around the world. Immigrants have won half of the nation's Fields Medals (for outstanding achievement in mathematics) and a large share of the nation's Nobel Prizes, and they are roughly twice as likely as native-born Americans to start a new business. Sixty percent of the most highly valued technology companies today were founded by immigrants to the United States or the children of immigrants, and in 2014, one-quarter of new engineering and technology start-ups had an immigrant founder.[15] eBay, Intel, and Google were all founded or cofounded by immigrants (respectively, Pierre Omidyar, Andy Grove, and Sergey Brin).

In 2017, all U.S. investment in R&D—from public and private sources—totaled $496 billion, more than in any other country. American universities dominate the global list of educational institutions advancing science, inventing new technologies, and spurring new sectors.[16] Private-sector investment and R&D continue to be robust, driving new waves of invention and commercialization. Business R&D increased from $70 billion in 1980 to $300 billion in 2016, a 340 percent rise (see figure 4).[17] U.S. technology companies significantly outspend their competitors on R&D. In 2017–18, U.S. firms, led by Amazon and

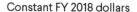

Figure 4. U.S. R&D FUNDING BY SECTOR

Constant FY 2018 dollars

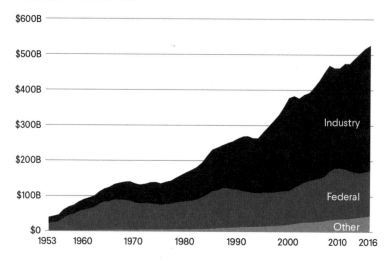

Source: American Association for the Advancement of Science.

Alphabet (Google's parent company), invested more than $5 in R&D for every $1 spent by Chinese companies.[18]

Moreover, the total amount of venture capital (VC) invested in U.S.-based companies has risen from $14.5 million in 1980 to $131 billion in 2018.[19] The United States attracted more than half the global investment in seed-stage funding (funding that supports proof of concept or early product development), followed by China. The United States leads the world in providing business, financial, and information services, and despite the rise of China, U.S. technology companies are the largest producer of high-technology manufacturing, with 31 percent of global share (though recently American companies have moved more of their production offshore).[20] In short, the U.S. innovation system retains great strengths.

> U.S. leadership in science and technology is at risk because of a decades-long stagnation in federal support and funding for research and development. Private-sector investment has risen, but it is not a substitute for federally funded R&D directed at national economic, strategic, and social concerns.

U.S. innovation leadership is not guaranteed. Public spending on basic science drives discoveries that would have been too big and risky for a private company to undertake. In effect, federal investment funds R&D with national economic, strategic, and social returns, while private-sector R&D is motivated by commercial returns. Moreover, public R&D creates spillovers that benefit the entire economy and incentivize greater R&D funding in the private sector. Yet despite its importance to the nation's innovation base, federal spending on research and development as a percentage of the overall economy has declined since the mid-1980s, from 1.2 percent of GDP in 1985 to 0.66 percent in 2016 (see figure 5).[21]

The end of the Cold War hastened this downward trend, as did the budget sequestration in the aftermath of the 2008 financial crisis, which mandated deep cuts to federal spending, including federal R&D. (However, research spending received a boost during the crisis, through the American Recovery and Reinvestment Act.) Federal R&D as a percentage of the budget peaked at close to 12 percent in the mid-1960s because of the Apollo space program but declined in the years after its end, to close to 3 percent in 2017.[22] The main lever to increase research spending would be to reverse the long-term decline in overall domestic discretionary spending, since federal spending on civilian research as a percentage of domestic discretionary spending has been relatively steady over the last decades.

The private sector is becoming the largest funder of research, with respect to not only commercially viable applied research but basic R&D as well. In 2015, for the first time since World War II, the federal government provided less than half of all funding for basic research.[23] But the private sector invests a much smaller share of its revenues in riskier, early-stage basic and applied research than in later-stage development.

Figure 5. U.S. R&D FUNDING BY SECTOR AS A SHARE OF GDP

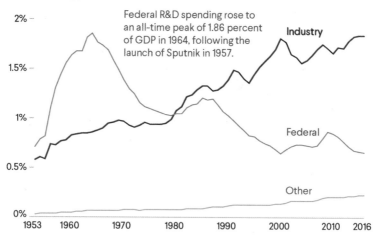

Percent of GDP

Federal R&D spending rose to an all-time peak of 1.86 percent of GDP in 1964, following the launch of Sputnik in 1957.

Industry

Federal

Other

Source: National Science Foundation.

In the past, corporate research laboratories such as Bell Labs and IBM Research made early-stage investments in translating basic science into products. Corporations now face short-term market and shareholder pressures to focus on incremental advances in existing technologies. They are not funding research and development that leads to new breakthroughs in science and engineering and spurs commercial growth later.

President Trump came into office with the intention of cutting the federal budget, and he has repeatedly proposed deep reductions to nondefense R&D spending, as well as to overall domestic discretionary spending. Congress has rejected these cuts, instead passing an omnibus spending bill in 2018 that provided the largest increase in R&D funding in nearly a decade, made possible by a significant increase in the cap on domestic discretionary spending and on defense spending.[24] The president's 2020 budget request has again proposed sharp reductions in R&D funding, including a 13 percent cut to the NSF, a 12 percent cut to the NIH, and the elimination of Advanced Research Projects Agency-Energy, a program that funds speculative environmental technologies.[25]

The Task Force believes the Trump administration is failing to provide the long-term leadership in R&D required to protect U.S.

prosperity and security. The White House needs to recognize the urgency of the innovation challenge and reach an agreement with Congress on the budget caps for fiscal years (FY) 2020 and 2021.

Trade Disputes' Disruption of Innovation

> Friends, allies, and collaborators tightly link technology ecosystems and create scale in a globalized system of innovation, and thus are a competitive advantage. Washington's current trade policies needlessly alienate partners, raise costs for American tech firms, and impede the adoption of U.S. technology in foreign markets.

The Task Force warns that the Trump administration's indiscriminate use of tariffs against China, as well as partners and allies, will harm U.S. innovative capabilities. The White House has rightfully targeted Beijing's market-manipulating policies and theft of intellectual property as central issues in the bilateral relationship. But extensive tariffs on Chinese information and communications technology (ICT) products will increase component costs for U.S. companies, leaving them less money for their own U.S. ICT investment, and will thus lower productivity and slow the growth of output by perhaps $163 billion over the next ten years.[26] The tariffs also disproportionately target imports of intermediate inputs—products American companies purchase to combine with other materials to place in final products and then sell globally. As a result, U.S. goods are more expensive and thus less competitive against those of other producers. The trade wars also impede the adoption and deployment of American technologies in foreign markets, as Canada, the European Union, Mexico, Russia, and Turkey have all retaliated against American exports.[27]

Moreover, Trump's declaration that trade disputes with friends and partners are based on national security threats and his willingness to enter into intensive trade battles with friends and adversaries alike have undermined alliances and thus weakened efforts to change China's behavior. Asian and European partners are also concerned about China's technology threat and the erosion of their industrial base. The European Commission's March 2019 review of the EU's relations with

China, for example, criticizes Beijing for "preserv[ing] its domestic markets for its champions, shielding them from competition through selective market opening, licensing and other investment restrictions; [and] heavy subsidies to both state-owned and private sector companies."[28] U.S. tariffs on products from friends complicate, if not make impossible, any effort to build a broad coalition and simultaneously make it easier for Beijing to play trading partners against each other.

The Trump administration erred in withdrawing from the Trans-Pacific Partnership (now known as the Comprehensive and Progressive Agreement for Trans-Pacific Partnership, or CPTPP). Joining the CPTPP, a trade deal covering twelve countries and close to 40 percent of the global economy, would have strengthened U.S. leadership in Asia and increased leverage on Beijing. China would have faced pressure to conform to CPTPP trade rules in order to attract investment, and leaving the agreement weakened U.S. credibility with its Asian allies.[29]

The United States has also gradually been decentered in global scientific and technology networks. This is due partly to the rise of Brazil, India, and other hubs of scientific discovery. But China is also competing with the United States for the roles of funder and partner, promoting scientific collaboration as part of the Belt and Road Initiative (BRI), its effort to connect to the Indian Ocean, Persian Gulf, and Europe. The Chinese Academy of Sciences, for example, has invested almost $268 million as part of the BRI and opened nine research and training centers in Africa, Central Asia, South America, and South and Southeast Asia.[30]

The Narrowing Talent Pipeline

A central strength of the U.S. innovation environment has been a steady pipeline of domestic STEM talent and the country's ability to attract the best and brightest students, engineers, and scientists from around the world. A lack of strong education initiatives at home and new barriers to talented foreign students' and workers' coming to and remaining in the United States will have long-term negative economic and national security consequences.

The United States is also seeing a decline in its ability to attract highly educated immigrants, and the number of new international students enrolling at American institutions fell by 6.6 percent during the 2017–18 academic year, after a 3.3 percent decline the year before.[31] These decreases have been driven by increased competition from other countries for talent, as well as by U.S. gun violence, public safety fears, and concern about restrictive immigration policies. Recent policy decisions, such as two 2017 executive orders banning travel to the United States for citizens from seven Muslim-majority countries, have complicated scientific exchange. These travel restrictions have disrupted researchers' plans, and a number of technology conferences, such as a meeting of the Internet Engineering Task Force, have been rescheduled to venues outside the United States to allow foreign participation.[32]

Actions by the Trump administration to limit H-1B visas have hampered tech firms that rely on top global talent to staff their operations. The denial rate for applicants trying to extend their visas grew from 4 percent in 2016 to 12 percent in 2018 to 18 percent in the first quarter of 2019.[33] The administration has also proposed ending the work authorizations for H-4 visa holders (the spouses of H-1B visa holders), making it yet more difficult to retain talent. In addition, in June 2017, the Department of Homeland Security (DHS) proposed ending the International Entrepreneur Rule, which provides temporary residency to foreign entrepreneurs starting a business in the United States. Other countries, such as Australia and Canada, are using these developments to lure talent. In a 2019 survey of four hundred U.S. hiring professionals from big and small companies, 63 percent said they were increasing their presence in Canada, either by sending more workers there or by hiring foreign nationals, because of U.S. immigration policies.[34]

In May 2019, the White House announced a new merit-based immigration plan, which would replace the family-based system of green card issuance with a Build America visa favoring workers with "extraordinary talent," "professional and specialized vocations," and "exceptional academic track records." The changes could result in up to 5,340 more immigrants with a master's degree or higher getting visas.[35] Even if the plan were to gain support in Congress, which currently looks unlikely, the Task Force does not believe the Build America visa effectively addresses the global talent race since it does not allow immigrants highly skilled in tech to bring their families with them. Very few skilled workers will come to the United States without their families when they can choose similar opportunities in Australia, Canada, or the United Kingdom and keep their families together.

Concerns about whether the United States itself is producing enough scientists, engineers, and technologists date back to Sputnik and the competition with the Soviet Union, and have reemerged almost every decade since. Today, an increasing percentage of college graduates major in STEM fields, but significant shortfalls remain in government and industry in specific sectors such as cybersecurity, mechanical engineering, systems engineering, and aerospace engineering.[36] U.S. universities are currently projected to produce fewer than 30 percent of the required number of graduates to fill the 1.4 million computer specialist job openings. Moreover, a smaller number of these students are American citizens, as the proportion of foreign students studying STEM subjects in the United States has doubled in the last thirty years. One estimate is that given current trends, international students will make up half of all STEM doctorates by 2020.[37]

It is important to note that the United States is not fully utilizing American talent, either. Minorities and women remain underrepresented in STEM fields. Only 2.2 percent of Latinos, 2.7 percent of African Americans, and 3.3 percent of American Indians and Alaska Natives hold a university degree in STEM fields.[38] Women constitute 47 percent of the overall workforce but only 28 percent of the science and engineering workforce, and women in tech jobs leave the field at a rate 45 percent higher than men.[39] More inclusive environments not only would address talent shortages and inequality of opportunity, but also are essential to economic and national security since they are demonstrated to be more innovative.[40]

The National Innovation Security Base

The Defense Department and the intelligence community will fall behind potential adversaries if they do not rapidly access and deploy technologies developed in the private sector.

The accelerating pace of innovation and the importance of private-sector R&D have strong implications for national security. Many of the technologies that are central to U.S. military predominance over peer and near-peer competitors—precision munitions, unmanned aerial systems, and other technology-enabled capabilities deployed in the past eighteen years—emerged from research sponsored by the federal government. The Pentagon funded almost 50 percent of the research and development in semiconductors from the 1950s until the 1970s. The shift to the private sector began in the 1980s, and by 1999 the Defense Science Board Task Force on Globalization and Security noted that the Defense Department was "relying increasingly on the U.S. commercial advanced technology sector to push the technological envelope and enable the Department to 'run faster' than its competitors."[41]

Today, the Defense Department cannot remain ahead of potential adversaries without access to an expanded pool of technologies developed in the private sector. Technology companies innovate the software, computational capabilities, data analytics, and processing speed that drive the leading edge of cyber, space-based, unmanned, autonomous, and other complex military systems. While the DOD's research, development, test, and evaluation (RDT&E) budget increased from $37 billion to $66 billion, or roughly 175 percent, over the past four decades, global R&D spending increased more than 1,875 percent during a similar period.[42] In 2015, the top four U.S. defense contractors combined spent only 27 percent of what Google does annually on R&D.[43] This gap has only widened (see figure 6).

Many of the tech sector's new advanced technologies are multiple-use, benefiting both economic and military power. There are interconnections between the private sector's investing in and developing these technologies and the military's using them, but the private sector and military are governed by different rules and frameworks. Moreover, the defense base is national, while technology companies operate globally. The Defense Department has no monopoly on new technologies, as they are increasingly available to all nations, including U.S. competitors. As a result, competitive advantage derives from identifying emerging technologies and fielding complex systems more quickly. The 2018 National Defense Strategy notes, "Success no longer goes to the country that develops a new fighting technology first, but rather to the one that better integrates it and adapts its way of fighting."[44]

The U.S. military services have difficulty capitalizing on new technological developments in the private sector because of inflexible capital allocation and acquisition processes. As the 2018 strategy points out, the Defense Department "is over-optimized for exceptional performance at the expense of providing timely decisions, policies, and capabilities to the warfighter." The battle systems of the future are software intensive, but bureaucracies designed to prevent waste and corruption are poor matches with a software development process that is iterative and where the end product is often unknown.

An April 2019 study on software acquisition by the Defense Innovation Board (DIB), an independent advisory committee to the DOD, concludes that "a large amount of DOD's software takes too long, costs too much, and is too brittle to be competitive in the long run."[45] Most DOD software projects adopt a "waterfall" development process that involves forming requirements, taking bids, selecting contractors, and then executing programs so they meet the listed requirements. The whole process can take so long that when the software is eventually deployed, it no longer matches operational needs. In addition, the Pentagon runs many closed proprietary and legacy systems, such as the Strategic Automated Command and Control System, which runs on a 1970s-era IBM computer system, and the Computerized Movement Planning and Status System, which uses Windows 2008.[46] Systems like these are expensive to maintain and force operators and warfighters into costly, time-consuming work-arounds. The DIB report warns

*Figure 6. U.S. TECH COMPANIES OUTSPEND
DEFENSE CONTRACTORS ON R&D*

Largest R&D budgets in 2018

All U.S. firms

Amazon	$22.6B
Alphabet	$16.2B
Intel	$13.1B
Microsoft	$12.3B
Apple	$11.6B

U.S. defense contractors

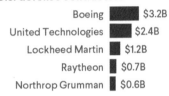

Boeing	$3.2B
United Technologies	$2.4B
Lockheed Martin	$1.2B
Raytheon	$0.7B
Northrop Grumman	$0.6B

Source: PwC.

that if the Pentagon "does not take steps to modernize its software acquisition and development practices, we will no longer have the best military in the world, no matter how much we invest or how talented and dedicated our armed forces may be."

The DOD is only now adapting to start-up businesses, which require faster decisions and smaller funding increments. The economic incentives for start-ups to partner with the government are, however, mixed. Entrepreneurs must navigate complex bureaucracies and contracting processes. Most venture-backed companies are expected to start earning revenue within eighteen months, but it can take the Defense Department two years to award a contract, followed by testing, approval, and prototyping. In that time, the original technology may have also changed. Early-stage ventures thus often focus on the commercial sector, with its more reliable revenue and shorter sales cycles.

Not everything, of course, can "fail fast." Weapons platforms that involve large numbers of warfighters in the loop, such as airplanes, submarines, and ships, will always demand longer development times, exceptional performance, and steady oversight. The challenge for lawmakers and Pentagon leaders is to balance risk and supervision appropriately.

In-Q-Tel, a venture capital firm established by the Central

Intelligence Agency, has been investing in start-ups with defense- and intelligence-related technologies since 1999. A number of more recent efforts have been made to shift portions of the Defense Department's procurement and deployment process closer to the funding models of the tech sector. DARPA's Cyber Fast Track program, now closed, opened up R&D competitions to start-ups and hackers, who rarely worked with the DOD. The program awarded 130 contracts at an average cost of nearly $150,000 between two and sixteen days after first proposal.[47] The Defense Innovation Unit (DIU), created in 2015, has opened offices in Austin, Boston, and Silicon Valley to develop relationships with technology ecosystems and streamline procurement processes. In its first years, DIU awarded sixty-five contracts worth $200 million in the areas of artificial intelligence, autonomy, human systems, information technology (IT), and space.[48] DIU has also fostered the growth of software and hardware companies seeking specifically to serve the Defense Department. These are welcome efforts that should now be bolstered and expanded.

A Shortage of Tech Talent in Defense

> The defense community faces severe challenges in attracting and retaining tech talent.

The armed services and Pentagon face a severe shortfall of talent in software development. They also often lack commercial cloud computing, agile software development environments, common machine-learning platforms, and other digital infrastructure with which coders are accustomed to working.[49] For example, in 2017 the Air Force had approximately 400 enlisted airmen and zero officers formally coded in the software development career field, out of roughly 320,000 uniformed Air Force members. Technical specialization is rarely good for career advancement in the military. The 2019 DIB report on software acquisition notes that "talented software developers and acquisition personnel with software experience are often put in jobs that do not allow them to make use of those talents, particularly in the military where rotating job assignments may not recognize and reward the importance of software development experience."

A number of programs have tried to develop new technology talent within the Defense Department. Kessel Run, an Air Force project supported by DIU and involving a partnership with Pivotal Labs, has trained seventy airmen in software and application development.[50] The Defense Digital Service (DDS) recruits individuals from private technology companies for a limited tour of duty with the Pentagon. Jyn Erso, run out of the DDS, pairs talent from the private sector with the army's top technologists, including in Army Cyber Command.[51] DDS is a small program, having grown from roughly a dozen staffers to close to seventy in 2019, and relies on temporary personnel. These programs are a good start, but much more is needed. The lack of a direct career path for those with technical skills in the services and the insistence on training talent internally rather than hiring top external experts remain major obstacles in recruiting and retaining talent.[52]

The Challenges of Hardware

The defense community faces deteriorating manufacturing capabilities, insecure supply chains, and dependence on competitor nations for hardware.

In addition to its software and talent problems, the Defense Department also faces complications in hardware innovation. Many of the sectors that Chinese manufacturers hope to dominate, and that the Chinese government supports through industrial policies, are the same as the DOD's research and engineering priorities. U.S. manufacturers, like their international competitors, create their most cutting-edge hardware products from complex supply chains that span the globe. Critical design functions and high-end components are generally produced in the more advanced economies of the United States, Germany, Japan, South Korea, Taiwan, and others, with most of the IP and talent remaining—and growing—in those locations. Much of the final assembly of the components happens in China. Beijing is actively seeking, both through its own companies and through interaction with global multinationals, to encourage more valuable parts of the value

Drone Manufacturers

The U.S. experience in commercial drones reflects some of the risks of Silicon Valley's current focus on software development. The American company 3D Robotics was an early player in the field, but a variety of missteps led to a loss of market share to the Shenzhen, China-based DJI Technology, which slashed prices and quickly developed new products. Notably, 3D Robotics relied on contract manufacturers, whereas DJI was designing and manufacturing every product itself. As one 3D Robotics manager put it, "We realized . . . it's just going to be inherently much more difficult for a Silicon Valley-based, software-focused company to compete against [a] vertically integrated powerhouse manufacturing company in China."[53] DJI now accounts for 70 percent of the commercial unmanned aerial system market. There are now no major U.S. drone manufacturers, only lower-end Chinese drones, and Parrot, a French firm. Parts of the U.S. military have banned use of DJI because of security concerns.

chain to occur within its borders, or, when they are overseas, through supply chains that allow China to control or access the most relevant intellectual property.

Skills have also been lost from the domestic workforce since 2011, when the Budget Control Act required sequestration of $109 billion, affecting both mandatory and discretionary spending. Defense spending has increased since then, but the lack of predictable funding during that period led to the loss of roughly seventeen thousand defense vendors. The overall result has been deteriorating manufacturing capabilities, insecure supply chains, and a high level of dependence on competitor nations.[54] Policymakers, in consultation with the private sector, need to develop a more sophisticated view of global supply chains. Specifically, for critical technologies they should delineate which parts of the value chain are the highest priority for the United States: which components should be manufactured within the United States, which are most important for its companies to lead regardless of location of activity, and which would be most troubling to cede to

Chinese companies or international companies operating in China.

High-tech start-ups are unlikely to fill the hardware innovation gap on their own. Companies built around hardware face high risk in terms of technology development and high costs associated with building research facilities, attracting scientific expertise, and manufacturing. The average amount required for a first funding round (known as Series A) for hardware companies is between $5 and $20 million, and subsequent rounds can reach as high as $50 to $100 million. The average Series A investment in a software-based company is between $1 and $3 million. Given the smaller risks of investing in software, VC firms funnel the vast majority of their investments to software, resulting in a funding gap for hardware. In 2017, 92 percent of U.S. VC dollars—up from 55 percent in 2006—went toward software-based technologies that have lower capital requirements, less invention risk, and quicker returns. Unless support for hardware manufacturing increases, the United States will rely increasingly on foreign companies that produce abroad, including in China.

A Persistent Divide

A persistent cultural divide between the technology and policymaking communities threatens national security by making it more difficult for the Defense Department and intelligence community to acquire and adopt advanced technologies from the private sector and to draw on technical talent.

Addressing the Defense Department's hardware, software, and talent shortcomings is made more difficult by a persistent cultural divide that has been deeply exacerbated by some genuine policy differences and the current domestic political environment. This fissure has historical precedent. Draper Laboratory was spun off from the Massachusetts Institute of Technology (MIT) and became an independent research organization after protests from students and scholars about research in support of the Vietnam War. The current divide emerged over which uses of surveillance and encryption are legitimate, with the technology companies often siding with global users' privacy concerns over the needs of intelligence and law agencies.[55] The divide has widened as employees at several of the largest technology companies have protested the use of artificial intelligence, facial recognition, and other frontier technologies for defense, intelligence, and homeland security projects. Engineers at Google, for example, pushed the company to cancel participation in Project Maven, an artificial intelligence project with the Pentagon, and to refuse to bid on the Defense Department's Joint Enterprise Defense Infrastructure (JEDI) project, a $10 billion IT improvement program.[56] As it was distancing itself from Washington, Google was developing Dragonfly, a censored search engine for the Chinese market.

In effect, Defense Department officials see the United States as in an emerging arms race with China over AI and other technologies and have expressed concern about the role U.S. companies are playing in Chinese technology development. General Joseph F. Dunford Jr., chairman of the Joint Chiefs of Staff, noted the troubling implications of the behavior of some U.S. companies: "I have a hard time with companies that are working very hard to engage in the market inside of China, and engaging in projects where intellectual property is shared with the Chinese, which is synonymous with sharing it with the Chinese military, and then don't want to work for the U.S. military."[57] U.S. companies have much more complex views that vary enormously by company. Most see China as a huge market opportunity critical to their evolving supply chains; but they also see Chinese firms as fierce competitors and state-sponsored threats to their intellectual property. The growing presence of Chinese firms in Silicon Valley has deepened these views.

Despite these public contretemps, a fair number of technologists are willing to work with the U.S. government. In a February 2019 BuzzFeed survey of one thousand tech workers in Silicon Valley, 59 percent of respondents "somewhat agree" or "strongly agree" that "tech companies should work with the U.S. government on military projects," whereas only 31 percent of tech workers "somewhat agree" or "strongly agree" that U.S.-based tech companies should operate in China.[58] Top executives at Amazon and Microsoft have also affirmed their willingness to work on classified contracts for the military and the intelligence community, while others, including Apple, build products that are already in use there.[59]

The Task Force believes that closing the divide between policymakers and the tech industry is essential to national security. It will require greater transparency, explanation, outreach, and experimentation by the Defense Department, as well as increased interaction between members of the military and technology communities. In addition, tech leaders should frequently and publicly explain to their employees that they have the best chance of shaping the development and use of frontier technologies by working with the Pentagon directly.

China and the Rise of the Rest

China is investing significant resources in developing new technologies, and after 2030 it will likely be the world's largest spender on research and development. Although Beijing's efforts to become a scientific power could help drive global growth and prosperity, and both the United States and China have benefited from bilateral investment and trade, Chinese theft of intellectual property and its market-manipulating industrial policies threaten U.S. economic competitiveness and national security.

The pressure on the United States is heightened by the rise of other science and technology competitors, especially China. Countries in Asia and Europe have steadily improved their innovation ecosystems, rolling out R&D tax incentives and increasing government funding for research and technology commercialization initiatives. In 1960, the United States accounted for 69 percent of global R&D. By 2018, the United States' share had fallen to a little over 25 percent, with 43.6 percent of the spending emanating from Asia.[60] Japan, Singapore, South Korea, and Taiwan have all seen science and technology as essential to economic security. Seoul, for example, increased spending on R&D as a percentage of GDP from 2.1 percent in 2000 to 4.5 percent in 2017.[61]

China in particular has ambitious plans to become a world leader in science, technology, and medicine. Between 1991 and 2015, China increased its R&D expenditures thirtyfold, averaging an 18 percent increase annually since 2000.[62] In nominal terms, Chinese

R&D expenditures rose to $254 billion in 2017, approximately 45 percent of U.S. R&D spending for that year. Adjusted for purchasing power, China's R&D expenditures were closer to 88 percent of U.S. spending.[63] China's GDP is growing and China is dedicating a greater portion of its economic resources to R&D, planning to eventually reach a spending target of 2.5 percent of GDP. It will likely equal or exceed the United States in overall R&D expenditures after 2030 (see figure 7).

The STEM workforce in China has also rapidly expanded. The total number of Chinese universities grew from 1,792 to 2,560 between 2005 and 2015. Eight million Chinese students graduated from college in 2017, compared to approximately 1.9 million graduating with bachelor's degrees and 1 million with associate's degrees in the United States.[64] The number of science and engineering bachelor's degrees conferred in China increased from 359,000 in 2000 to 1.65 million in 2014.[65] China surpassed the United States as the world's largest producer of natural sciences and engineering doctorates in 2007.[66] Questions have been raised about the quality of some Chinese programs, but there is no doubt that the Chinese ability to compete in STEM fields has grown (see figure 8).

In addition, with ambitious science projects, generous salaries, and high levels of lab funding, China has made a concerted effort to recruit top foreign talent.[67] The Thousand Talents Program offers scientists a one-million-yuan ($151,000) starting bonus and research funds of three to five million yuan. Foreign scientists receive additional incentives, such as subsidies for accommodation, visits home, and education.[68] The Department of Energy recently warned that talent programs were offering scientists at U.S. national labs hundreds of thousands, and in some cases millions, of dollars to conduct research in China.[69]

Figure 7. COUNTRIES' R&D SPENDING

Bubbles represent countries, positioned according to R&D spending as a percentage of GDP and sized according to total R&D spending.

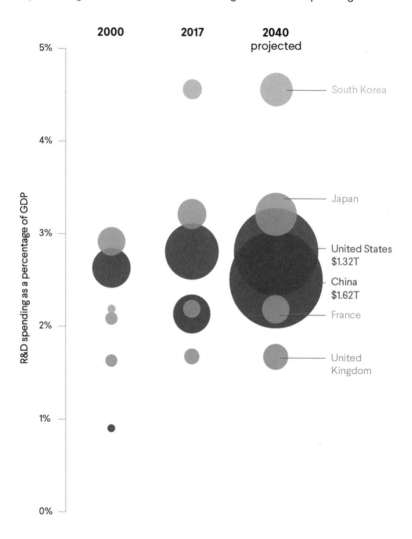

Note: The projection assumes that, except for China, countries' R&D spending as a percentage of GDP will remain at 2017 levels. China's R&D spending is projected to increase to 2.5 percent by 2023, according to the Chinese government's stated goal.

Source: OECD.

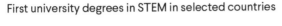

Figure 8. U.S. AND CHINESE STEM GRADUATES

First university degrees in STEM in selected countries

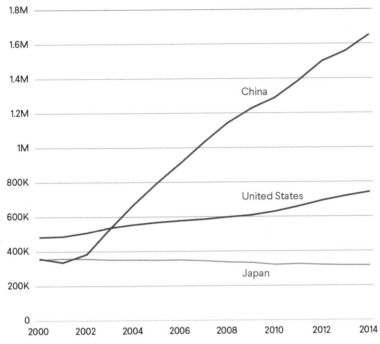

Source: National Science Board.

China is closing the technological gap with the United States, and though it may not match U.S. capabilities across the board, it will soon be one of the leading powers in technologies such as AI, robotics, energy storage, 5G, quantum information systems, and possibly biotechnology.

This increase in spending and STEM personnel is beginning to pay off in scientific accomplishments. China overtook the United States in the production of scientific papers in 2016. According to a study by scientific publisher Elsevier and business news outlet Nikkei, China published more high-impact research papers than the United

States did in twenty-three out of thirty research fields with clear technological applications. China has built many of the world's fastest supercomputers and will likely beat the United States to building the first exascale supercomputer, despite investing around the same amount in supercomputers as the United States.[70] China's current five-year plan prescribes that the biotechnology sector should exceed 4 percent of GDP by 2020, and state, provincial, and local governments have invested more than $100 billion in the life sciences sector.[71] BGI (formerly the Beijing Genomic Institute) is by some measures the largest genome-sequencing center in the world, and an increasing number of U.S. companies depend on Chinese partners to do their sequencing and analysis. China also plans to build the largest-ever particle accelerator. In 2016 it became the first country to send a quantum-encrypted message via satellite, and in 2018 it held the first quantum-encrypted video call. In January 2019, China became the first country to land a vehicle on the far side of the moon.

China has three industrial policies designed to raise its innovation capabilities: the 2014 Integrated Circuit (IC) Promotion Guidelines, Made in China 2025, and the Next-Generation Artificial Intelligence Development Plan. The IC Promotion Guidelines, an attempt to build an indigenous integrated circuit industry, involves investments reportedly between $100 and $150 billion in public and private funds. The goal is to have Chinese firms produce 70 percent of the chips consumed by Chinese industry, reducing their dependence on U.S., Korean, and Taiwanese suppliers. Made in China 2025 sets ambitious targets for upgrading China's aging manufacturing base through smart manufacturing and offers low-interest loans from state-owned investment funds and development banks, assistance in buying foreign competitors, and extensive research subsidies.

On AI, Beijing hopes to leverage massive amounts of data, permissive regulations, entrepreneurial firms, and government support to build an industry worth $150 billion by 2030. In 2017, China's AI industry received nearly $26 billion in investment and financing.[72] The United States still leads in cutting-edge R&D, specialized chips, and talent, but China surpassed the United States in volume of AI research in 2014, including in AI-related patent registration and articles on deep learning. China is also training a large number of specialists.[73] Twenty-three percent of the accepted papers for the 2017 Association for the Advancement of Artificial Intelligence conference were from China, rising from only 10 percent in 2012, and AI authors in China were cited 44 percent more in 2016 than they were in 2000 (see figure 9).[74] China

Figure 9. CHINESE UNIVERSITIES RISING IN ARTIFICIAL INTELLIGENCE FIELD

Universities ranked by publications in top AI conferences. Chinese universities are in red.

2014 rankings

1. Carnegie Mellon University
2. Tsinghua University
3. Technion - Israel Institute of Technology
4. Massachusetts Institute of Technology
5. University of Michigan
6. University of Toronto
7. University of Alberta
8. Ben-Gurion University
9. Cornell University
10. Georgia Institute of Technology
11. University of Texas, Austin
12. University of Oxford
13. University of Southern California
14. Stanford University
15. University of California, Los Angeles

2018 rankings

1. Carnegie Mellon University
2. Tsinghua University
3. Stanford University
4. University of California, Berkeley
5. Peking University
6. University of Oxford
7. Georgia Institute of Technology
8. University of Massachusetts, Amherst
9. ETH Zurich
10. Massachusetts Institute of Technology
11. University of Texas, Austin
12. Chinese Academy of Sciences
13. Cornell University
14. Nanjing University
15. Nanyang Technological University

Source: MacroPolo, Paulson Institute.

will open around four hundred majors related to data science, artificial intelligence, and robotics in universities in 2019.[75]

Although Chinese companies have smaller R&D budgets than their American competitors, they are world leaders in a number of frontier technologies. The country's two largest internet companies—Alibaba and Tencent—have developed highly innovative e-commerce and mobile payment platforms. Datang, Huawei, and ZTE own about 10 percent of 5G-essential intellectual property rights (IPR), and many analysts expect China to fully commercialize 5G by 2020, five years ahead of the United States, Australia, the EU, Japan, and South Korea (see figure 10). Officials at Huawei announced that they planned to more than double annual R&D spending to between $15 billion and $20 billion, which would place the company between second and fifth place in worldwide spending on R&D.[76] Chinese companies such as Baidu, ByteDance, Face++, iFLYTEK, and SenseTime are driving the

Figure 10. CHINESE FIRMS DOMINATE 5G ROLLOUT

Market share of base stations in 2017. Chinese firms are in red.

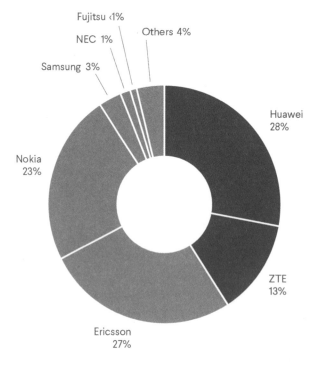

Fujitsu ‹1%

NEC 1%

Others 4%

Samsung 3%

Huawei 28%

Nokia 23%

ZTE 13%

Ericsson 27%

Source: *Nikkei Asian Review.*

application of AI to voice and facial recognition software, autonomous vehicles, and internet content. In the first and second quarters of 2018, the volume of Chinese VC investment surpassed that of the United States for the first time.[77]

Civil-military fusion is a pillar of Chinese military modernization and an effort to bolster the country's innovation system for advanced multiuse technologies in aviation, aerospace, and information technology. Introduced by then President Hu Jintao in 2009, the effort to bridge the gap between the civilian industrial base and the military has intensified under President Xi Jinping. Within his first year in office, the Central Committee voted to elevate civil-military fusion to a national strategy, and in January 2017 Xi created the Central Commission for Integrated Military and Civilian Development, a high-level decision-making and coordination body for civil-military fusion efforts. The top seven state funds dedicated to investing in civil-military fusion industries report having over 362 billion yuan ($56.85 billion) in capital.[78] Civil-military fusion plays a prominent role in both Made in China 2025 and the Next-Generation Artificial Intelligence Development Plan. Beijing's policies could help it achieve a meaningful edge in the development of future weapons systems, reducing or perhaps eliminating a longstanding source of strategic advantage for the United States.

China also seeks to influence the digital infrastructure of the future through the Belt and Road Initiative. Along with investment in railways, roads, pipelines, and ports along the route, Chinese companies plan to build a "digital Silk Road": fiber-optic cables, mobile networks, satellite relay stations, data centers, and smart cities. ZTE, for example, operates in over fifty of the sixty-four countries on the route of the Belt and Road Initiative. It lays fiber-optic cables; sets up mobile networks; and provides surveillance, mapping, cloud storage, and data analysis services to cities in Ethiopia, Laos, Nigeria, Sri Lanka, Sudan, and Turkey.[79] Beijing hopes these economic ties will translate into political influence over the shape of the internet and the rules governing emerging technologies.

The Chinese innovation model is not without its own weaknesses. China spends only about 5 percent of its R&D funds on basic research, compared to 17 percent in the United States.[80] Chinese firms depend on American technology in some critical areas, especially semiconductors. Top-down direction and industrial policy often leads to waste, corruption, and redundancies. Plagiarism and fabrication of scientific results are perennial problems at Chinese universities and research labs. Although an increasing number of foreign-trained Chinese scientists are returning home, they often find that the research environment is hierarchical and grants depend on political and personal connections. Moreover, the Chinese Communist Party is now reasserting political control over technology companies, which for the last decade benefited from a relatively laissez-faire environment. This may slow the introduction of new products and innovation.

The Chinese leadership is aware of these barriers to innovation and is beginning to address them. Chinese officials have also interpreted U.S. efforts to cut off the flow of technology to Huawei and other companies as an effort to contain China's rise as a science and technology power. They have responded by doubling down on innovation and self-reliance, with the objective of reducing their dependence on U.S. technology, especially in the semiconductor and semiconductor-tool industries.[81]

The challenge from Beijing is pressing and immediate, but the United States needs to look beyond China, and beyond competition over a specific list of cutting-edge technologies. There is much that Washington can and should do that is unrelated to Beijing and is instead concentrated on maintaining U.S. leadership. The U.S. government, the private sector, and academia should work together to increase the national capacity for scientific and technological innovation and accelerate the adoption and deployment of new technologies by defense and intelligence agencies.

The Trump Administration's Innovation Agenda

> Although the Trump administration has boosted the budgets of several technology-related organizations within the DOD and issued a number of executive orders, its efforts to accelerate innovation in critical frontier technologies such as AI are too incremental and narrow in scale.

The Task Force commends the Trump administration for bringing much-needed attention to innovation issues and for shining a spotlight on the development of critical technologies such as 5G and AI. However, the White House has not taken on the challenges in a comprehensive way that will produce durable results. Despite bipartisan support for broad technology competition with Beijing, the White House has failed to work with Congress to increase federal support for basic R&D and has adopted an incremental and limited approach to supporting the development of frontier technologies. The White House's immigration policies have weakened the country's ability to compete for talent, and unnecessary trade conflicts with friends and allies have hampered the building of international technology coalitions and could slow innovation.

The Trump administration's innovation strategy has combined a commitment to deregulation with a number of executive orders in support of frontier technologies, the expansion of broadband, and workforce development.[82] Administration officials have stressed that while the federal government has a role to play in making important investments in R&D, it is the private sector that drives innovation, and thus a large focus should be on removing regulatory barriers that slow American entrepreneurs. In March 2017, Trump established the White House Office of American Innovation (OAI), which aims to streamline government and cut red tape. The office's remit is relatively narrow, given the scope of the innovation challenge, and in its first years it focused on two information technology initiatives: publishing a report on IT modernization and creating the Centers of Excellence program to drive agencies to the cloud and better data management.

The Trump administration has, however, also pushed for a more muscular government response in areas where it sees innovation as a matter of great-power competition. The White House's FY 2019 budget called for increasing funding for RDT&E of new technologies in the Defense Department to its highest level since the end of the Cold War. The majority of this funding increase would support late-stage development, prototyping, and testing activities.[83] The administration requested a $360 million increase to DARPA's funding in FY 2019, to $3.432 billion from $3.07 billion in FY 2018, and an additional $125 million, to $3.556 billion, in FY 2020.[84] The Defense Innovation Unit saw a nearly trifold increase in its budget under the administration's FY 2019 budget, from $29.6 million to $71 million, which then more than doubled to $164 million in FY 2020.[85] The Task Force strongly encourages these important signals of continued support for two innovative organizations within the DOD, but the scale remains small compared to the massive Defense Department budget.

The Trump administration has also increased its focus on cutting-edge technologies such as semiconductors, quantum computing, and artificial intelligence. In 2017, DARPA launched the $1.5 billion, five-year Electronics Resurgence Initiative to support work on advanced chip design and manufacturing. In September 2018, the White House held the Summit on Advancing American Leadership in Quantum Information Science, at which the Department of Energy announced $218 million in funding and the National Science Foundation $31 million to support multidisciplinary quantum research. Trump signed the National Quantum Initiative Act in December 2018, which authorizes the government to provide $1.2 billion to fund activities promoting quantum information science over an initial five-year period. These are all positive steps, but they are incremental and fairly limited in scope. To truly meet the innovation challenge, a much broader and more sustained approach on multiple fronts—including federal investment in R&D, a moonshot approach to innovation policy, comprehensive immigration reform, and partnerships with friends and allies—will be needed.

> The United States is ahead of the rest of world in AI, but others are closing the gap—and U.S. failure to compete for global talent could result in the loss of its lead.

The Task Force is concerned that the White House has been slow in driving the development of AI, failing to build immediately on the Barack Obama administration's release of a national AI plan in 2016.[86] A growing number of governments have introduced national strategies: Canada, China, Denmark, the EU Commission, Finland, France, Germany, India, Italy, Japan, Mexico, the Nordic-Baltic region, Singapore, South Korea, Sweden, Taiwan, the United Arab Emirates, and the United Kingdom have all released strategies to promote the use and development of AI.

In response to this criticism, officials note a steady stream of actions on AI during 2018 and 2019. The FY 2019 National Defense Authorization Act (NDAA) created the National Security Commission on AI, which has been tasked with assessing the national security implications of AI. In June 2018, the Pentagon announced the Joint Artificial Intelligence Center (JAIC), which will partner with industry and academia to help the DOD utilize AI. The FY 2019 NDAA includes $70 million in funding for the center.[87] DARPA has committed to a multiyear $2 billion investment in new and existing programs, in its AI Next campaigns.[88]

The White House also held a summit in May 2018 with industry representatives to discuss AI policies and announced that federal agencies would make data available for private-sector AI research.[89] It established a new Select Committee on AI, housed under the National Science and Technology Council and including representatives from DARPA, the NSF, and the OSTP. The committee will advise the president on government priorities in AI and build private-sector partnerships.

On February 11, 2019, Trump signed an executive order enabling the American AI Initiative.[90] A day later, the Defense Department released its AI strategy, designed to accelerate the delivery and adoption of AI; strengthen partnerships with industry, academia, allies, and partners;

cultivate an AI workforce; and lead in military AI ethics and safety.[91] Along with the executive order, the White House issued a National Security Presidential Memorandum, "Protecting the United States' Advantage in Artificial Intelligence and Related Critical Technologies," which charges the assistant to the president for national security affairs with coming up with a plan to protect the United States' advantage in AI from strategic competitors and foreign adversaries.

These efforts, however, are inadequate. Action does not match the language officials use to describe the importance of AI to U.S. economic and national security. The American AI Initiative provides no new sources of federal support and is unclear about how much the government should be spending on AI research and development. Individual agencies are told to "budget an amount for AI R&D that is appropriate for this prioritization," but without additional funding, they will need to shift funds, leaving other research areas underfunded. Lacking any specific spending goals, the initiative has no ability to measure whether an agency is adequately prioritizing AI research. Few details were given for the initiative's execution.[92]

Huawei and 5G

In the race for the next generation of communications technologies, the Trump administration has developed only a few parts of what should be a multifaceted strategy. It has failed to coordinate a response to Huawei's global expansion, muddied its message about the company's economic and national security risks, and not sufficiently accelerated domestic efforts to deploy 5G.

5G will offer data speeds up to fifty or one hundred times faster than current telecom networks and will serve as critical infrastructure for AI, automated vehicles, the Internet of Things, and other industrial sectors. In October 2018, Trump signed a memorandum directing the Commerce Department to develop a long-term, comprehensive national strategy for spectrum (that is, radio waves, which are used in telecommunications) and ordering federal agencies to review their existing spectrum usage, forecast future demands, and prepare a plan for research and development that will enable better use of spectrum in the future.[93] In April 2019, the Federal Communications Commission (FCC) announced the third, and largest, auction of high-frequency spectrum for 5G—opening up use of high-frequency spectrum to companies so they can roll out 5G commercially—and a $20 billion fund to expand broadband in rural areas.[94]

In addition, the Trump administration has moved to block Chinese telecom firms from rolling out 5G in the United States and foreign markets. In May 2019, Trump signed two executive orders to that effect. The first authorized the Commerce Department to block U.S. companies from using telecom equipment and services from companies controlled by "adversary governments." U.S. officials have claimed the order is "agnostic," but it has been widely interpreted as being directed at China and Huawei.

The second order has larger consequences for the company. It ordered the Commerce Department to place Huawei and sixty-eight affiliates on a list of companies to which U.S. firms may not sell components without government approval. Broadcom, Intel, Qualcomm, and Xilinx stopped working with Huawei after the order was announced, and Google stated that it would no longer provide the Android mobile operating system and apps for Huawei's smartphones. Cut off from U.S. chip and software suppliers, Huawei's ability to operate—and its future—were highly uncertain. Huawei founder Ren Zhengfei has said he expected company revenues to decline by $30 billion over the next two years because of U.S. actions.[95] During the June 2019 Group of Twenty summit in Japan, however, Trump agreed to lift some of the sanctions against Huawei, allowing sales of widely available components made by American companies.[96]

The White House and the State Department have also, with mixed results, tried to convince other countries not to use Huawei and other Chinese telecommunications equipment in their next-generation wireless networks. While Australia, Japan, and New Zealand have banned Huawei, other friends and allies are moving ahead, despite threats from the United States to limit intelligence sharing. Most notably, officials in France, Germany, and the United Kingdom have argued that they can manage security risks by developing strict standards, inspecting equipment and code, and installing Huawei equipment only on peripheral, controlled networks.[97]

The Task Force believes the White House was right to publicize the security risks of Huawei and block adoption of the company's equipment in U.S. networks. The use of the Commerce Department list to ban sales to Huawei, however, was too blunt an instrument and caused significant blowback for U.S. technology companies. It has also encouraged China, and others, to reduce dependence in areas where American technology companies dominate, such as semiconductors and design tools.

Moreover, Trump's willingness to overturn the sanctions on Huawei suggests that the sanctions were based on U.S. economic interests rather than legitimate security risks, which undercuts efforts to convince other countries to exclude the company. Senator Marco Rubio (R-FL) tweeted that a reversal on Huawei would be "a catastrophic mistake" that would "destroy the credibility of [the Trump] administrations warnings about the threat posed by the company, no one will ever again take them seriously."[98]

Technology Protections

> Beijing has often exploited the openness of the American system. Efforts to protect U.S. intellectual property are a necessary complement to, but not a substitute for, innovating faster than China. The administration is over-weaponizing trade and investment policy, with costs to U.S. innovation.

The campaign against Huawei has at times overlapped with a major facet of the Trump administration's innovation strategy: protecting American technology at home and abroad. In August 2018, Congress passed the Foreign Investment Risk Review Modernization Act (FIRRMA), which broadens the jurisdiction of the Committee on Foreign Investment in the United States (CFIUS), allowing it to investigate, and possibly block, more foreign deals. The Committee may now investigate a foreign entity buying not just an entire company but also minority, noncontrolling investments. The Trump administration has blocked the sale of Lattice Semiconductor to a group that involved a Chinese venture capital firm; barred Broadcom's $121 billion offer for Qualcomm; prevented Ant Financial's acquisition of MoneyGram; and demanded that Beijing Kunlun Tech give up control of Grindr.

Total Chinese direct investment in the United States has fallen 90 percent, to $5 billion last year from $46 billion in 2016, driven in part by FIRRMA but mainly by tighter controls on outward investment from Beijing.[99] The legislation is beginning to affect early-stage investments: some capital has moved into new sectors that are not as politically sensitive, and some dealmakers in Silicon Valley say Chinese funds are looking for deals outside the United States to avoid scrutiny.[100] American venture capital firms are reportedly dropping their Chinese investors or walling them off, and some start-ups have forced out Chinese investors to avoid regulators.[101] In April 2019, PatientsLikeMe, a health-care start-up, was ordered to find a new buyer after the Trump administration forced its Chinese majority shareholder to divest its stake.[102] Once the new rules are fully implemented, the drop-off could be even more noticeable.[103]

It is not only the inflow of money that has provoked security concerns. The size of the Chinese student population in the United States—an estimated 350,000, about half of whom are studying at the undergraduate or lower levels—presents a challenge to law enforcement and counterintelligence agencies. FBI Director Christopher Wray and other U.S. officials have recently warned that Chinese intelligence is using expatriate scientists and students to gain access to technologies at universities and businesses.[104] The FBI, federal granting agencies, and members of Congress have signaled that universities need to do more to prevent foreign actors from attempting to steal intellectual property.[105] In June 2018, the State Department implemented a one-year limit on visas for Chinese graduate students studying in sensitive research fields, with the chance to reapply every year. The administration is reportedly considering new background checks and other restrictions on Chinese students.[106]

The White House is also deploying new export controls to slow the pace of Chinese development. The Commerce Department is developing regulations to restrict "emerging and foundational technologies," including robotics, 3-D printing, and biotechnology, as well as several categories of AI, including computer vision, speech recognition, and natural language understanding.[107] In June 2019, the Commerce Department prohibited U.S. chip companies from selling to five Chinese entities involved in developing exascale computing, including the supercomputer maker Sugon.[108]

The United States is also trying to pressure Beijing into ending the theft of IP and trade secrets from U.S. companies. Presidents Xi and Obama had signed an agreement in 2015 to refrain from economic espionage, but Chinese hackers have returned and targeted numerous corporations, including cloud providers and IT service suppliers.[109] In November 2018, then Attorney General Jeff Sessions announced the China Initiative, to identify priority trade-theft cases, pool Department of Justice and FBI resources to combat Chinese economic espionage, and evaluate whether additional legislative and administrative authorities would be required to protect U.S. assets from foreign economic espionage.[110] Between October and December 2018, the Department of Justice unsealed indictments three times against Chinese intelligence officers and hackers for the theft of U.S. businesses' IP and trade secrets.[111]

The Task Force commends the White House for confronting China on cyber espionage and IP theft. Updating CFIUS and export controls is also overdue, especially in the case of Sugon, which has connections to China's People's Liberation Army. The Task Force warns, however, that the administration is over-weaponizing trade policy, with long-term costs to U.S. innovation capabilities. The issue is not only the loss of revenues to U.S. tech companies from Chinese customers, though these are significant. It is also that Beijing and others will want to reduce dependence on U.S. high-tech supply chains now that they have seen them leveraged for political goals.

The Task Force believes investment restrictions and export controls are a necessary but secondary part of any strategy responding to China's rise as a science and technology power. As such, limitations on the flow of people and money should be drawn as narrowly as possible. Slowing China down is not as effective as outpacing it. The United States needs its own innovation policies.

RECOMMENDATIONS
Restore Federal Funding for Research and Development

Most of the technology breakthroughs underlying U.S. economic and military strength have drawn on federally funded R&D, with work carried out in federal laboratories, universities, and industry. Sufficient federal investment in research is vital to advancing national goals in the areas of health, defense, and the economy. The United States cannot rely on its private sector to make the type of investments in large-scale, risky research projects that lead to new discoveries and breakthroughs in science and engineering. Addressing the challenge from China and other rising science powers requires an ambitious plan of national investment in science and technology.

The White House and Congress should restore federal funding for research and development to its historical average. This would mean increasing funding from 0.7 percent to 1.1 percent of GDP annually, or from $146 billion to about $230 billion (in 2018 dollars). Only the government can make the type of investments in basic science that ignite discoveries; such investments are too big and risky for any single private enterprise to undertake. The heads of the Department of Defense, Department of Energy, NASA, National Institutes of Health, National Science Foundation, and other agencies should submit budgets that restore funding of basic research to historic average levels and maintain it. (For the DOD, this would be "6.1 funding," meaning basic, as opposed to applied or advanced, research.)

Maintaining these levels of spending is essential. The sustainability of funding for basic research over predictable time spans is as important as raising the total amounts of support. Funding needs to be protected from political as well as budget instability. The Trump administration's recent reversal on fetal tissue research, for example, is likely to disrupt existing projects and cause delays in launching research programs. China, India, Singapore, and the United Kingdom all conduct research using fetal tissue.

Federal and state governments should make an additional strategic investment in universities. The investment, of up to $20 billion a year for five years, should support cross-disciplinary work in areas of pressing economic and national security interest. The federal government should commit this investment toward a sustained program at universities of supporting fundamental research targeted at critical technologies. Working with academia and the private sector, the federal government should identify national priorities for innovation. These may include AI, machine learning and data science, quantum information systems, personalized medicine, and clean energy. The program should include substantial new funding for research, targeted scholarships and fellowships, fabrication and test-bed facilities, and financing for start-ups. The funding should encourage cross-disciplinary work and simplified university-industry partnerships, with specific plans to bring advances to market.

State governments should provide public research universities with sufficient autonomy. They should also restore and maintain per-student funding for higher education, including public research universities, to the mean level for the fifteen-year period from 1987 to 2002 (adjusted for inflation).

The White House should announce moonshot approaches to society-wide national security problems. This would support innovation in foundational and general-purpose technologies, including AI and data science, advanced battery storage, advanced semiconductors, genomics and synthetic biology, 5G, quantum information systems, and robotics.

Often, the U.S. policy default is to unleash the private sector through deregulation and tax reform. Deregulatory actions are certainly required in many sectors. The United States ranks fifteenth in the OECD in terms of the frequency in which it updates its regulations, and seventeenth in regulatory quality by the Global Innovation Index.[112] Patchwork regulations, high compliance costs, and regulatory complexity slow, for example, the development and deployment of autonomous vehicles, blockchain and financial technology, and commercial drones.

But deregulation on its own cannot cope with both the scale of disruption and the intensity of the challenge from other countries,

China in particular. Beijing melds top-down industrial policy and massive state investment with strong commercial actors and an entrepreneurial culture. Based on the current state of AI development, China's ability to combine data collection and analysis across health, industrial, internet, and mobile sectors may give it a competitive advantage in the design of algorithms and the development of machine learning. In addition, Chinese tech firms operate in a blurred space between the state and the private sector, and many of their ambitious technology goals are inherently multiuse, with strategic implications for economic and national security. Defense against Chinese techno-nationalism, transfer of intellectual property, and cyber espionage is necessary but far from sufficient to ensure American technological success. As it has in the past, the United States needs to go on the offense to advance its own technological capabilities.

The United States should not replicate the Chinese model, but the current policy approach is too narrow in scale, uncoordinated, and incremental. The Task Force recommends a moonshot approach to industrial policy, an approach the United States has followed in the past. Special interagency subcommittees representing a number of government agencies and working with academia and the private sector should be organized to coordinate the selection, development, and execution of R&D programs that address society-wide and pressing national security problems such as threat detection networks; commercial, gate-based quantum computers; and carbon-capture technologies. Partnered federal agencies—for example, the NIH and NSF—would provide catalytic R&D support for these multidisciplinary projects, with firms and academic institutions collaborating and cooperating with one another on precompetitive innovation projects. In technology areas with less immediate commercial interest and weak industry investment, the government should fund research and coordinate early purchases.[113]

Address the AI and 5G Challenges

Two of the technologies high on the Trump administration's agenda require a more comprehensive and urgent approach: AI and 5G. The Office of Science and Technology Policy should request additional funding, drawn from the increase in federal spending, for AI research and development, and, working with Congress and industry, it should outline clear metrics of success and accountability. The United States continues to lead in the specialized chips essential to AI development, and, through DARPA, the National Institute of Standards and Technology (NIST), and the NSF, the federal government should fund precompetitive basic research in AI hardware. OSTP, in consultation with academia and industry, should form a plan for a national AI R&D workforce.

Federal agencies also need to develop sector-specific AI strategies.[114] The Department of Commerce, for example, could oversee a network of institutes that would advance AI in manufacturing, including the participation of industry, academia, and government agencies. The NIH could partner with universities and the private sector on applying machine learning to speed clinical diagnosis, treatment, and therapies.

One of China's competitive advantages in AI is centralized access to data. U.S. policy should be directed at moving more data from the public sector into shared—but secure and protected—data sets. All government agencies should increase access to government data sources in machine-readable formats. Relevant federal agencies should support the development of shared pools of high-quality, application-specific training and validation data in areas of public interest such as agriculture, education, health care, public safety and law enforcement, and transportation, after ensuring that appropriate privacy protections are in place.[115] In January 2019, Trump signed the Open, Public, Electronic, and Necessary (OPEN) Government Data Act, which requires all nonsensitive government data to be made available in open and machine-readable formats by default, but the mandate is unfunded.[116] The federal government should also consider creating a National Discovery Database that would allow access to data at scale for problems of unique interest to national security. While considering the potential ethical and privacy challenges involved, state and local governments should also study making nonsensitive data available for use in AI systems.[117]

Any successful strategy will require the right regulatory framework. Congress should pass federal privacy legislation that is technology neutral (i.e., that allows companies to adopt the technology that is most appropriate to achieve objectives) and begins by defining obligations and processes for organizations that process data. Perhaps most important, given the U.S. lead in AI talent, the Task Force calls on the administration to ensure that the United States remains the most attractive location for data scientists and engineers by following the recommendations for talent below.

The United States faces a future where Chinese telecom companies

Semiconductor Industry

The U.S. government has in the past taken more active responses to new technological competitors. Between 1978 and 1986, for example, the U.S. market share for dynamic random-access memory (DRAM) fell from 70 to 20 percent, while the Japanese share jumped to 75 percent. Tokyo promoted production through government-sponsored research; long-term, low-cost loans; and technology transfers. In order to sell into the market, IBM and Texas Instruments had to share technology with Japanese partners.

U.S. policymakers saw the challenge from Tokyo as both an economic and a security threat, and saw a domestic semiconductor industry as essential to American military strength. The Semiconductor Research Corporation was founded in 1982 as a nonprofit research consortium of thirty-six companies and federal government agencies designed to promote basic research and ensure a steady flow of graduate students with interest and experience in semiconductors. At the time, there were big scientific questions about the future of semiconductors, and the industry was unwilling and unable to conduct the basic research needed for future innovations. Early research centers were established at Cornell University, Carnegie Mellon University, and the University of California, Berkeley. Five years later the Semiconductor Industry Association founded Sematech, a nonprofit consortium to solve common manufacturing problems. DARPA provided five years of funding worth $500 million.[118]

In a January 2017 report, the President's Council of Advisors on Science and Technology recommended a similar industrial-policy approach to semiconductors. The approach would be meant to strengthen research and innovation in the U.S. semiconductor industry in response to China's industrial policies to build its own capabilities. Suggested moonshots included research in areas such as biothreat detection, weather forecasting, and quantum computers.

deploy a large part of global 5G infrastructure and services.[119] China has already made $180 billion in capital expenditures for 5G deployment over the past five years, installing about 350,000 5G-operable base stations, nearly ten times the number currently deployed in the United States.[120] Huawei has emerged as a major player in the global supply base for this equipment, while U.S. and European firms have either contracted in size or exited the market entirely. Huawei has signed forty contracts to sell 5G equipment and has shipped seventy thousand base stations to Africa, Asia, Europe, and the Middle East.[121]

China's dominance poses economic and security risks for the United States. As an April 2019 DIB report on the 5G ecosystem argues, "The leader of 5G stands to gain hundreds of billions of dollars in revenue over the next decade, with widespread job creation across the wireless technology sector." Moreover, future 5G networks built on Chinese equipment "would pose a serious threat to the security of DOD operations and networks going forward."[122] Leadership in the next generation of wireless connectivity is an economic and national security concern.

As the DIB report notes, the world leader in 5G is unlikely to be the United States, in part because no American companies manufacture the equipment to transfer signals between mobile phones and the towers or sites that make up the network.[123] This reality highlights a longer-term lesson for Washington stressed throughout the Task Force report: policymakers need to provide greater incentives for R&D and domestic manufacturing in technology areas judged to be critical to national security. They also need to block mergers and acquisitions that could lead to equipment being supplied only by a limited number of foreign companies.

In the near term, the United States will need to coexist with Huawei, because many other countries have made it clear they will not follow Washington and implement a complete ban. Hobbling Huawei is not, however, a substitute for meaningful efforts to accelerate the deployment of 5G in the United States. U.S. companies dominated the apps for smartphones and other services provided over 4G, and they can do the same for 5G if it is deployed rapidly. U.S. spectrum policy is, however, focused on the high-band wavelength, making 5G communications slower and more expensive to roll out compared to Chinese and European efforts. The FCC should repurpose mid-band spectrum for new wireless applications and free up low-band spectrum held by the federal government, particularly the DOD. The federal government should also work with municipalities and states to speed small-cell deployment with the goal of accelerating penetration.[124]

In addition, as part of its investment in universities, the federal government should fund several 5G R&D centers at universities in areas where the United States might lead, including security and merging communications, storage, and computation in 5G. Those centers should also begin research into 6G technologies that are likely to roll out fifteen years from now and experiment with public-private partnerships to develop, license, and commercialize new intellectual property.[125]

Huawei is supported by government subsidies, has a guaranteed share of the Chinese domestic market, and is innovative both in its products and its business. It has thus been able to offer its services and products at prices significantly lower than its European competitors, Ericsson and Nokia.[126] Washington has been trying to convince other countries that they should pay more for greater security, but many have rejected the U.S. risk assessment. For those who do see a threat from Huawei, the United States will need to make these European suppliers more affordable. The United States should, through the U.S. International Development Finance Corporation, provide loans or loan guarantees for telecommunications equipment in developing economies.

For those U.S. allies and partners unwilling to adopt a blanket ban on Chinese telecom companies, Washington should work with them to develop shared standards for inspecting and deploying 5G equipment, similar to the joint statement issued by thirty countries in Prague, Czech Republic, in May 2019.[127] Washington should also work with allies such as Japan and the United Kingdom on supply-chain security reviews. Secretary of State Mike Pompeo and other State Department officials have threatened close allies with the loss of intelligence sharing if they do move ahead with Huawei; but this would be counterproductive and endanger U.S. security, since information does not flow just one way.[128] In addition, as the Defense Innovation Board argues, the U.S. military should assume that wireless networks dominated by Chinese suppliers are vulnerable to cyberattacks and plan for resiliency and added layers of redundancy.[129]

Attract and Educate a Science and Technology Workforce

The nations with the best talent will push to the farthest edges of the science and technology frontier. Talent has been at the foundation of U.S. technological prowess, and the United States' ability to attract the best and the brightest from around the world has provided a competitive edge for most of the last half century. This edge is now at risk.

The United States cannot stand still as others devote new resources to developing human capital. Educational analysts deem a substantial percentage of STEM programs in China to be not of equivalent quality to their American peers, but the absolute number of graduates—1.65 million Chinese science and engineering graduates in 2014, compared to 740,000 in the United States—leads to a strength of its own.[130] Government, universities, and the private sector need to cooperate to expand the STEM pipeline and support new pathways into technology and science careers.

The White House, Congress, and academia should develop a twenty-first-century National Defense Education Act, with the goal of expanding the pipeline of talent in math, engineering, and the sciences. A twenty-first-century NDEA would support up to twenty-five thousand competitive STEM undergraduate scholarships and five thousand graduate fellowships. It would also increase the number of graduate fellowships and traineeships supported by existing programs at federal science and education agencies, including the Departments of Defense, Education, Energy, and Homeland Security; NASA; the National Institutes of Health; and the National Science Foundation. For example, Congress and the administration should expand the DOD National Defense Education Program, which provides scholarships and fellowships to students in critical fields of science, mathematics, and engineering in return for a commitment of national service after their studies.

Universities, federal and state governments, and businesses should address the underrepresentation of minorities and women in STEM fields through mentoring, training, research experience, and academic and career advising. They should also provide financial support for room and board, tuition and fees, and books, as well as assessments of job placement opportunities in STEM fields, highlighting employers with clear track records of fairness in hiring, promotion, and pay. The Meyerhoff Scholars Program at the University of Maryland, Baltimore County, which is one of the largest pipelines for doctorates in science and engineering among African Americans, is one initiative that provides these types of support; it also encourages collaborative coursework and cutting-edge lab work. Effective strategies to promote inclusion of women students, scientists, and technologists include on-campus childcare centers, equal opportunities for women and men to lead committees and research groups, mentoring programs to reduce the isolation of women faculty, and pauses in the tenure clock for up to one year for raising children. Within the workplace, flexible, collaborative environments that offer leadership development, mentoring, and networking for women are linked to higher rates of retention. Workplaces that employ women in higher levels of management are more able to attract and retain women at lower levels of employment.

Federal agencies, the private sector, and universities should work together to support debt forgiveness for students going into specialized technology sectors. The Cybersecurity Talent Initiative, launched in April 2019 by MasterCard, Microsoft, the Partnership for Public Service, and Workday, guarantees graduates in cybersecurity-related fields a two-year placement in the CIA, DOD, DOE, FBI, or another federal agency. Afterward, graduates receive opportunities in the private sector and up to $75,000 in student loan assistance.[131] Similar programs should be developed in AI, quantum computing, and other specialized technologies.

The United States needs to make it easier for foreign graduates of U.S. universities in scientific and technical fields to remain and work in the country. Congress should "staple a green card to an advanced diploma," granting lawful permanent residence to those who earn a STEM master's degree or doctorate. Congress should also pass the DREAM Act, which would provide undocumented immigrants who were brought to the United States as children an expedited path to citizenship if they accomplish academic goals or serve in the military. The administration should reverse measures that have created new obstacles for many foreign students and foreign workers on temporary work visas, such as the H-1B.

Congress should pass legislation that permits immigrants to live and work in the United States if they can raise funds to start new companies. Many immigrants trying to start businesses are also recent graduates of U.S. universities. The Startup Act, which has bipartisan support, would create an entrepreneurial visa to permit seventy-five thousand immigrants annually to remain temporarily in the country if they have raised enough capital to launch a new company, and to remain permanently if the company succeeds.

The federal government should make targeted—rather than sweeping— efforts to prevent the theft of scientific knowledge from American universities. Foreign graduate students bring great expertise to American higher education and are essential drivers of new discoveries. Foreign undergraduate students are often a lucrative source of funding for many universities. Broad bans on Chinese students would hurt U.S. innovation. They would also reinforce a sense among Chinese scientists and students that the bans are motivated by racial hostility, allow the Chinese government to position itself as a protector of Chinese abroad, and thus reinforce Chinese Communist Party propaganda that equates Chinese heritage with the party.[132] Some technologies are more sensitive than others, and graduate students are more likely to have access than undergraduates. The most effective measures to stop theft will likely be tighter controls over technology in universities and research labs, accompanied by expanded counterespionage efforts.

Universities should be more proactive in offering proposals on tightening controls over sensitive technologies. They also need to enforce existing rules on disclosure of foreign funding and limits on the transfer of research findings and intellectual property. Congress should provide the FBI with greater resources so agents can review students on a case-by-case basis and zero in on those who trigger significant concern. The ultimate goal should be retaining the openness of the U.S. research system and the longstanding exemption of fundamental research from controls and limitations, enshrined in the Ronald Reagan administration's 1985 National Security Decision Directive 189.[133]

Support Technology Adoption
in the Defense Sector

The federal government, particularly the Defense Department, needs to move more rapidly to acquire and integrate breakthrough technologies. Processes and bureaucracies developed during the industrial age are not optimized for agility and speed. Moreover, peer and near-peer competitors, such as China, do not have the same legacy systems to overcome and can blur the line between public and private sectors through new industrial-military policies. Although moving to a flexible institutional culture more accepting of risk is a systemic process involving many parts, changes in two areas—finding and funding new technologies and talent circulation—will have a more immediate effect.

Notable experiments have been made with more flexible budget authorities and the consequent acceptance of more risk. For example, at a meeting at which start-ups pitched new ideas to the Air Force, the Air Force brought contracting and payment times down from ninety days each to under fifteen minutes; the contract involved was only one page. The Air Force awarded $3.5 million through a credit card swipe to fifty-one start-ups, half of which had never worked with the U.S. government before.[134]

These experiments, however, remain small and inadequate to the scale of the challenge. The Defense Innovation Board identifies eighty-one major software development programs in the DOD, with budgets totaling $17.9 billion. Credit card swipes are not going to be enough to change the Pentagon's acquisition process. Congress needs to find additional ways to help the DOD and other federal agencies find and exploit new technologies at scale in the private sector. Moreover, although senior military and intelligence leadership recognize the need to streamline bureaucracies and adopt a more risk-taking culture, this attitude has not taken hold in the bureaucratic middle, where many operational decisions are made and implemented.

Federal agencies and each of the military services should dedicate between 0.5 and 1 percent of their budgets to the rapid integration of technology. The heads of each agency should also hire a domain specialist deputy for fast-track technologies (for example, data sciences, robotics, and genomics) from outside the government for a two- to four-year assignment. This person would run a program similar to DARPA's Cyber Fast Track project in cyber and robotics, with an assigned budget to be used only for contract awards with nontraditional commercial partners and a goal of proposal to contract within an average of thirty days. Each agency would be expected to report outcomes, including reduced times to contract.

Congress should also allow the services to reprogram up to 10 percent of their budget in the same year. This flexibility would improve their ability to contract with nontraditional defense companies, including start-ups, which require faster decisions and smaller increments. The funds should champion the emerging defense-tech sector, which includes a new generation of software-driven defense contractors that are developing frontier technologies and want to work with the DOD but do not possess the scale of traditional defense firms. Congress, working with the services, would need to develop new methods of oversight for this high-risk portion of the budget, and the DOD would have to create a venture-oriented advisory board to provide advice on how to further accelerate adoption of advanced technologies from the start-up community.

Changes in budgeting need to be matched with changes in the way talent is developed and acquired. Although the more technologically advanced agencies, such as DARPA and NASA, have recruited and retained strong specialized talent, in general the government's ability to aggressively adopt new technologies is limited by the number and skill of technical people in government. The government is missing out on young talent. Data supplied by the Office of Personnel Management shows that at the end of FY 2017, less than 3 percent of full-time information technology professionals in federal agencies were under the age of thirty, while 51 percent were fifty or older.[135]

Congress should establish a new service academy, the U.S. Digital Service Academy, and a Reserve Officer Training Corps for advanced technologies (ROTC-T) to foster the next generation of tech talent. Like the other federal military academies, the new technology service academy would draw talent through a highly competitive process and congressional appointments; offer full scholarships; and require graduates to serve a period in national service, typically five years. Students would pursue studies in mission-critical technology areas such as AI, biotechnology, cybersecurity, data analytics, and robotics, and after graduation they would commission into either the services or the intelligence agencies, Department of Defense, Department of Homeland Security, or other government agencies as civil servants.[136]

Lifelong career paths should be complemented with more short-term, flexible options. The White House and Congress should bring people from the technology industry into all three branches of the government for temporary rotations. They should also develop new fellowships to encourage circulation of technologists, military officers, and federal officials between the technology sector and the Defense Department. For example, the U.S. Digital Service (currently approximately 185 staff members) and similar programs should be doubled in size. Scholars at Stanford University's Hoover Institution have suggested establishing a Technology Fellows Program that would select fifty of the most talented American engineering students graduating from college for a one-year, high-impact government placement in which they would work directly for senior leaders like the Air Force chief of staff, the secretary of defense, or the commander of U.S. forces in the Middle East.[137] An additional co-op–like program would enable technology graduate students to cycle through government as part of their training. Industry should define and adopt leave policies for civic service to allow tech talent to spend time in government, and technology companies should commit to hiring more veterans and those who have done public service to expose themselves to the national security worldview.

The Defense Department should also expand its programs that place military personnel at private companies. Currently, the Secretary of Defense Executive Fellows program places four or more officers or civilian employees each year in companies and corporations including Amazon, Apple, Google, Intel, and Salesforce. The program should be expanded, both in size and to smaller, less established companies to allow personnel to carry new skills back into their missions.

The Defense Department should maintain the Defense Innovation Board. In June 2019, Trump signed an executive order calling on federal agencies to evaluate advisory committees and terminate at least one-third of the current committees.[138] But the work of the DIB has been critical to identifying bureaucratic barriers to software development, technology acquisition, and innovation in the DOD as well as relaying high-level private-sector experience and expertise to Pentagon leadership.

In addition to tech expertise coming to policymakers, Washington should move to technology centers. Other agencies, as well as the armed services, should follow the examples of the Defense Department's Defense Innovation Unit, Department of Homeland Security's Silicon Valley Innovation Program, and National Geospatial Intelligence Agency's Outpost Valley in establishing locations in Austin, Texas; Boston, Massachusetts; and Silicon Valley, California, as well as other technology hubs such as Silicon Alley (New York City), Silicon Beach (Los Angeles), Silicon Prairie (the Midwest), and Silicon Slopes (Utah).[139] Government outposts like Sofwerx and Special Operations Works help ensure that eventual end users are involved in the acquisition and development process. They also allow for organizational experimentation: some will succeed in developing outreach to the venture capital and start-up communities and others will fail, allowing DOD leadership to learn what works.

Bringing tech talent into government is a means both to making federal agencies more agile and to shrinking the cultural and political divide between the two communities. Common ground between the technology community and the defense sector could also be found in a push for greater adoption of open-source technologies such as Linux, Hadoop, and Kafka in the defense world. Open-source software and the cloud have been a force multiplier for the consumer internet, providing the benefit of engineers contributing from around the world. The adoption of open-source technology in national security efforts has been slow, with Defense Department managers using and protecting legacy systems. Building open-source projects would not only bring greater efficiency to the Defense Department but would also provide opportunities for cultural cross-pollination.

Bridge building may also be easier when industry and the Defense Department both target transnational risks, such as cybersecurity or election interference. The DOD's AI strategy, for example, talks of forming "open missions" based on global challenges. Specifically, it suggests operationalizing AI for humanitarian assistance and disaster relief for wildfires, hurricanes, and earthquakes. Other federal agencies should look for similar projects that can energize the tech community around AI.

Bolster and Scale Technology Alliances and Ecosystems

In a globalized system of innovation, friends, allies, and collaborators are a competitive advantage. Assuming current rates of growth, China will pass the United States and become the world's largest funder of R&D sometime after 2030. But one of the great strengths of the U.S. innovation system is that it is a central node in a transnational network for turning ideas into new products. The United States does not need to outspend China dollar for dollar; it has a slew of alliances upon which it can call. Collaborative science and technology projects are central to long-term competitiveness.

The State and Treasury Departments should create a technology alliance to develop common policies for the use and control of emerging technologies. Membership would be made up of countries with shared concerns about the effects of frontier technologies on international stability and democracies, as well as those with significant technological capabilities. These include the members of the Five Eyes intelligence-sharing alliance (the United States, Australia, Canada, New Zealand, and the United Kingdom), Estonia, Germany, India, Israel, and Japan. At least in the first stage, membership would be limited to ten to fifteen countries to facilitate coordination of positions and development of concrete actions. The group would work to develop norms of state behavior in cyberspace and for AI governance. At issue is not only who will develop and deploy new technologies first, but also the values embedded within these new technologies and whether they will be used to reinforce or undermine democratic societies.

The technology alliance would also develop coordinated national export controls, defense trade controls, and investment review mechanisms to limit the transfer of multiuse technologies. Without support from other technology centers, export controls and investment restrictions will fail and likely damage U.S. commercial interests. European, Israeli, Japanese, and South Korean firms can be expected to replace American companies in selling to third markets. The Information Technology and Innovation Foundation estimates that new export controls could create losses of $14.1 billion to $56.3 billion in export sales over five years, depending on how restrictive the controls are and the degree of international coordination on stopping the flow of technology.[140]

The United States has a history of uneven results in regards to export controls on China when there is limited agreement on what technologies should be controlled. For example, over the last three decades, the United States has had tight controls on the sales of space technology to China, yet Beijing has become a space power, launching BeiDou, a domestic GPS system; supporting several manned missions to space; and landing a vehicle on the dark side of the moon. During this same time period, American companies' share of the commercial satellite industry fell from 83 percent in 1999 to 63 percent in 2005 and 40 percent in 2018.

The line around the next wave of disruptive technologies to be controlled should be drawn as finely as possible. For example, much AI research is done collaboratively by scientists around the world. High-tech companies share details of their work, with AI research papers published on sites like arXiv and code published on GitHub and other repositories.[141] Alliance partners will need to agree on distinctions between basic and applied research as well as commercial and military applications so that controls are as narrow as possible. Basic or fundamental research should not be subject to control.

To lead effectively in today's global technology innovation environment, the United States needs to base its technology and related national security strategy on an evolving view of global value chains. The national security legislative and regulatory framework of the United States and its tech alliance partners should address specific concerns related to potential adversaries' controlling supply chains associated with the design and production of sensitive hardware and software. The tech alliance should establish a clear set of priorities for both investment and defense to avoid wasting time and financial and political capital on technologies or value-chain activities that do not matter at the expense of those with concrete national security implications.

To assist with this effort, the White House should facilitate an ongoing dialogue among private-sector, academic, and government leaders to identify and categorize technologies that truly have national security implications if they fall into the wrong hands. Senators Mark Warner (D-VA) and Marco Rubio (R-FL) have introduced a bill to create an Office of Critical Technologies and Security in the Executive Office of the White House to coordinate policies designed to prevent the transfer of dual-use technologies, maintain U.S. technological leadership, and ensure supply-chain security.[142] Others have suggested better policy coordination through the Office of Science and Technology Policy. The goal of both efforts is to enable the creation and communication of a coordinated response across the government and to work with federal regulators, the private sector, state and local governments, and academia, as well as with international partners and allies.[143]

The Department of Commerce should work with major trading partners to promote the secure and free flow of data and the development of common technology standards. Cross-border data flows are essential to the modern digital economy. A 2016 McKinsey & Company report estimates that global data flows raised global GDP by approximately 3.5 percent over what it would have been without such flows.[144] Moreover, one of China's competitive advantages is the ability to mobilize massive pools of data across industries and uses. The movement and sharing of data among trade partners would allow their firms to achieve needed economies of scale.

But economic and political winds are now blowing away from data sharing. Skepticism and fears about how the major technology platforms collect and use data is high in the United States and Europe. More governments are promoting data-localization policies—regulations requiring companies to store and process data on servers physically located within national borders—in pursuit of privacy, cybersecurity, or economic advantage.[145] When the Trump administration withdrew the United States from the Trans-Pacific Partnership it restricted participants' ability to require data localization and firms to disclose source code, but the administration did secure similar protections for cross-border data flows in the U.S.-Mexico-Canada Agreement (USMCA).

Washington and its partners should look for common principles on privacy that would allow for the secure, privacy-protected flow of data in the near term, with a longer-term goal of developing new multilateral agreements. The United States can build on mechanisms already present in the Asia-Pacific Economic Cooperation forum and the U.S.-EU Privacy Shield agreement, which allow for national-level privacy protections and data transfer. USMCA's data provisions and protections of source code can also serve as a model. The U.S. trade representative should continue to promote protections for cross-border flows, source codes, and algorithms in all future trade agreements. In the absence of the CPTPP, Washington should also work with allies in the World Trade Organization (WTO) to pressure China to adhere to WTO rules and responsibilities and end discriminatory industrial policies.

Policymakers have also grown increasingly concerned about Beijing's efforts to shape standards in emerging technologies, especially 5G, AI, and the Internet of Things. In recent years, Beijing has issued hundreds of domestic standards, and Chinese technology companies have become more active and effective participants in international standards-setting forums.[146] The standards process in the United States has historically been industry-led, and Washington should not re-create Beijing's top-down, national-plan approach. But there may be technologies and international forums where U.S. companies could use additional government support. NIST should do a comprehensive study and suggest standards dialogues for emerging technologies where the federal government can play a more active supporting role.[147]

The Department of Commerce and the U.S. International Development Finance Corporation should encourage American start-ups in AI and data science, genomics and synthetic biology, quantum information systems, and other frontier technologies to invest in, export to, and form R&D partnerships with firms in emerging technology ecosystems. The goal would be fostering early adopters, developers, and customers who will build on U.S. technologies. Most innovation emerges from regional ecosystems made up of networks of technology firms, capital markets, and research universities. Over the last thirty years, new technology hot spots have emerged in places such as Bengaluru, India; Daejeon, South Korea; Durban, South Africa; Hsinchu, Taiwan; Lagos, Nigeria; Santiago, Chile; and Shenzhen, China. U.S. companies and venture capital firms have already developed connections to these hubs. In 1989, for example, U.S. multinationals conducted almost 75 percent of their foreign R&D in five countries: Canada, France, Germany, Japan, and the United Kingdom. By 2014, that number had dropped to 43 percent, with China, India, and Israel in particular becoming important new sources of talent and ideas.[148]

The Department of Commerce and the U.S. International Development Finance Corporation should develop targeted tax incentives and investment schemes to promote the closer linking of emerging technology hot spots. The goal is not only to accelerate innovation, increase revenues, and push forward product enhancement through the real-world use of technologies. It is also to encourage the adoption of U.S. technologies into these tech hubs and compete with Beijing's use of the Belt and Road Initiative to create export markets and demand for Chinese digital products. These efforts should be paired with incentives and investments from the federal and local governments to bolster technology corridors outside of Boston and Silicon Valley, in places such as Dayton, Ohio, and Huntsville, Alabama.

The Department of Energy, Department of State, National Institutes of Health, National Science Foundation, Office of Science and Technology Policy, and other relevant agencies should develop a network of international cooperative science and technology partnerships, open to governments and the private sector, to apply frontier technologies to shared global challenges, such as climate change. Federal agencies should not only fund efforts that will include cooperation with other nations' science organizations but should also provide R&D and tax incentives for tech firms to form international collaborative partnerships. In the past, the United States has used atomic energy, space exploration, agricultural production, and other collaborative technology projects as foreign policy tools. Scientists and scholars worked on projects that not only addressed pressing economic, health, environmental, and security challenges but also strengthened ties between the United States and its friends and allies. As Nina Federoff, former science advisor to Secretaries of State Condoleezza Rice and Hillary Clinton, noted, "Science by its nature facilitates diplomacy because it strengthens political relationships, embodies powerful ideals, and creates opportunities for all."[149]

Today, the United States should work with members of the technology alliance to develop projects in artificial intelligence and data science, advanced battery storage, advanced semiconductors, genomics and synthetic biology, 5G, quantum information systems, and robotics. An assistant to the president for science, technology, and global affairs in the OSTP should coordinate these plans. Technology firms and universities should provide guidance to ensure that the agreements serve strategic use and address global challenges. Federal agencies should set aside a percentage of their budget increases to fund efforts that will include not only cooperation with other nations' science agencies but also incentives for tech firms and universities to form international collaborative partnerships.

The DOD, as part of its effort to source innovative technologies, could also write contracts with companies in Australia, India, Japan, and other allies and partner nations. In 2017, Congress added Australia and the United Kingdom to the National Technology and Industrial Base, which oversees joint R&D and controlled technology transfer. The program, previously limited to the United States and Canada, should be further expanded to other technology alliance partners. Similarly, the Technical Cooperation Program, which currently involves collaboration among the United States, Australia, Canada, New Zealand, and the United Kingdom in research on areas such as electronic warfare and materials processing, should be expanded to other nations.[150]

When considering the scope of civilian collaborative R&D projects, U.S. policymakers should bear in mind that there are costs to painting all Chinese technological progress as a threat to the United States or its interests. The tech alliance should distinguish between competition over multiuse technologies with national security implications and more cooperative approaches to targeted technologies. Global challenges such as addressing climate change and stopping pandemics require technological collaboration, and all will benefit from breakthroughs in clean energy, carbon capture, and new vaccines against influenza. The alliance should include Chinese agencies, universities, and firms in a new multinational initiative that researches several targeted technologies, including carbon capture and storage, hydrogen fuel from renewables and water technologies, and technologies that make food supplies more resilient.

CONCLUSION

The United States has a long history of innovation, entrepreneurship, intellectual freedom, and openness. This innovation has powered the U.S. economy and allowed the U.S. military to overmatch potential adversaries. But the United States cannot expect the national security innovation base to automatically reset itself for the new demands of technology competition. Losing the technological edge the United States currently has over its competitors will impose significant risks. The next wave of breakthroughs will generate economic and military advantages for the countries that develop and deploy these technologies first.

Facing the threefold challenge of the accelerating pace of innovation, the diffusion of multiple-use technologies, and the rise of China, the United States must act now to build a national strategy for sustaining American leadership in innovation. As this report has detailed, this strategy has four pillars: restoring public support and funding for science, attracting and educating the world's best STEM talent, making rapid technological adoption a core competency in the Defense Department, and building an international technology alliance. The strategy will require rethinking traditional approaches to technology development. It will depend on government officials at all levels, the private sector, and universities working together to develop new forms of cooperation designed for agility and speed. In the end, it will require the United States to recommit to science and technology leadership and investment. With renewed dedication to a national innovation security strategy, the United States can ensure its continued and future economic growth and national security.

ADDITIONAL AND DISSENTING VIEWS

The National Laboratories, administered by the Department of Energy, are among the crown jewels of research in the United States. These seventeen labs began as a result of the increased funding for scientific research during World War II. The most well-known lab is Los Alamos, where the research into and development of the atomic bomb took place. But there is a long list of notable scientific and technical discoveries across all the labs, including the discovery of twenty-two chemical elements, the running of thirty-two of the five hundred fastest supercomputers, the provision of computational infrastructure for the Human Genome Project, and the development of GPS.[151]

Each year the National Labs receive roughly $12 billion in funding and produce nearly 1,500 inventions and 700 patents.[152] The labs also support the training of graduate students, with resources unavailable anywhere else, including supercomputers and equipment required to study high-energy physics, like advanced particle accelerators.

The effectiveness of the Trump administration's management and oversight of the labs has been called into question. It has recommended a 30 percent cut in funding for the National Labs. However, the labs' scientific track record continues to be strong, and cuts to funding would irreversibly harm the foundation these institutions provide to both national security and American technological competitiveness.

In line with this report's recommendations, funding to the labs should be increased. The Department of Energy should aggressively develop and recruit leaders to invigorate the National Labs with new models of research and continue to attract the best talent.

—DJ Patil
joined by Alana Ackerson, Steven A. Denning,
Laura D'Andrea Tyson, and Jerry Yang

The Task Force report keenly articulates the importance of bonds between the innovation and national security communities, but an additional emphasis on the human element is warranted. The growing civil-military divide, particularly in coastal technology hubs, has long-term implications for the United States' ability to compete. If its public- and private-sector leaders have not walked in one another's shoes, how can they navigate thorny issues such as the ethics of AI or collaborate closely in times of conflict?

This divide cannot be solved solely through business contracts, and the United States needs to restore opportunities for human connections between military members and technologists, with the hope that many of the latter will choose to serve in uniform for some period or at least maintain relationships with those who do.

Organizations like the Defense Digital Service and Defense Innovation Unit have done a tremendous job attracting civilians for short tours of service, but to operationalize innovation, the United States needs uniformed members to combine tech nativity with the authority inherent under Title 10.

Unfortunately, officer accessions from leading American computer science and engineering programs have dropped precipitously. In 1960, Stanford and MIT each graduated over one hundred ROTC members; today, they graduate less than a dozen per year. While these elite schools do not hold a monopoly on talent, it is concerning that the U.S. Armed Forces cannot attract a meaningful number of graduates from top institutions.

In 1980, 64 percent of members of Congress and 59 percent of Fortune 500 CEOs were military veterans. Today, those numbers have fallen to 19 and 6 percent, respectively. Military service in the United

States has become hereditary: according to the DOD's reporting, 80 percent of new recruits have veterans in their extended family and 25 percent have a veteran parent. Given that less than 1 percent of the U.S. population currently serves, the United States risks its military service being dominated by a narrow class of society; similar trends have historically not contributed to democratic stability. Further, most of the United States' military bases in major population centers, such as Chicago, Los Angeles, New York, and San Francisco, have been shuttered. As a result, nearly half of all military recruits hail from southern states.

If these trends go unchecked, the United States will lack the human bridges between innovation and national security necessary to maintain competitiveness. I submit two specific recommendations to renew those bridges:

1. Reopen military bases in technology centers, such as Boston and San Francisco. The human relationships between military families and their civilian neighbors are a powerful way of exposing technologists to the military and helping cut through false narratives. This is my personal story: I was the first in my family to join the armed forces, and the fact that I grew up in a town with a large air force base is not a coincidence.

2. Expand the size of the reserve component, including each branch's reserves and the Army and Air National Guard. The flexible career paths offered by the reserve component can be quite attractive for recruits who are interested in uniformed service but also have significant private-sector opportunities.

—*Raj M. Shah*
joined by Alana Ackerson and Steven A. Denning

Innovation is crucial to U.S. national competitiveness and national security. The United States needs to invest significantly more in research and development, and it must do so quickly. A moonshot approach linking greater investment to solving major societal challenges will both garner the necessary public support and foster the essential precompetitive partnerships among government, industry, and academia. One of these challenges is climate change, which is now recognized by the national security establishment as a major risk. The United States used a moonshot approach to respond to the Sputnik challenge and to win the race to the moon. Now it needs a moonshot approach to save the planet, and time is running out.

Climate change is another area of research in which the United States and China share common interests and can work together to defuse escalating tensions. China has become both a formidable economic competitor and a growing national security concern for the United States. China's goal is to become a global leader in transformative technologies like artificial intelligence, 5G, advanced semiconductors, and quantum computing, and to shape both the global economy and national security in the future. The United States can only succeed in mitigating the dangers posed by China's industrial policies if it innovates faster. Weaponizing restrictive trade and foreign investment policies may slow China's technological advance but will not stop it. Indeed, such an approach is likely to cause China to redouble its efforts to reduce its dependence on U.S. technology, and will certainly impose sizable costs on U.S. companies and the U.S. innovation ecosystem. Given the deep economic ties developed between the United States and China over the last thirty years, U.S. efforts to decouple the two economies to restrict China's technological rise should proceed with extreme caution, using only selective national security restrictions on trade and investment in targeted technologies deemed essential to national security. Such restrictions should be imposed not unilaterally but in cooperation with U.S. allies and through the WTO and other global institutions.

A smart competition policy with China should be a mixture of competition and cooperation.[153] During the Obama administration, the United States and China developed a constructive collaboration on climate change. Indeed, the success of the Paris Agreement was built on a bilateral U.S.-China agreement on carbon emissions targets. Tragically, the United States, by unilaterally withdrawing from the agreement, abandoned its leadership of the strongest current global effort to address the huge costs and risks of intensifying climate change and dismantled one of the most fruitful areas of U.S.-China research and technology cooperation. Fostering technological breakthroughs to stem climate change should be the focus of one of the cooperative technology partnerships or alliances recommended in this report, and the United States should invite China to participate.

Finally, it should be noted that for technologies deemed of critical importance to national security, a reliable supply chain is essential. For some products, that may mean that the United States will have to develop its own supply sources, in some cases relying on production in U.S. locations by U.S. companies or companies headquartered in allied countries. For technologies critical to national security, the United

States should rethink its reliance on dual-use or multipurpose technologies developed and produced by American multinational companies that are deeply embedded in global supply chains and depend on global production facilities and trade for significant shares of their global revenues.

—Laura D'Andrea Tyson
joined by Alana Ackerson, Steven A. Denning, and Jerry Yang

ENDNOTES

1.   For the growing debate on China policy see, for example, Kurt M. Campbell and Ely
     Ratner, "The China Reckoning: How Beijing Defied American Expectations," *Foreign
     Affairs*, March/April 2018, http://foreignaffairs.com/articles/china/2018-02-13/china-
     reckoning; Larry Diamond and Orville Schell, ed., *China's Influence & American Interests:
     Promoting Constructive Vigilance* (Stanford, CA: Hoover Institution, 2018), http://
     hoover.org/sites/default/files/research/docs/00_diamond-schell-chinas-influence-and-
     american-interests.pdf; Task Force on U.S.-China Policy, Orville Schell and Susan L.
     Shirk, ed., *Course Correction: Toward an Effective and Sustainable China Policy* (New
     York: Asia Society, 2019), http://asiasociety.org/sites/default/files/inline-files/
     CourseCorrection_FINAL_2.7.19_1.pdf; M. Taylor Fravel, J. Stapleton Roy, Michael
     D. Swaine, Susan A. Thornton, and Ezra Voge, "China Is Not an Enemy," *Washington
     Post*, July 3, 2019, http://washingtonpost.com/opinions/making-china-a-us-enemy-is-
     counterproductive/2019/07/02/647d49d0-9bfa-11e9-b27f-ed2942f73d70_story.
     html.

2.   See, for example, Robert Solow, "A Contribution to the Theory of Economic Growth,"
     Quarterly Journal of Economics 70 (February 1956): 65–94 and "Technical Change and
     the Aggregate Production Function," *Review of Economics and Statistics* 39 (August
     1957): 312–20; Paul Romer, "Endogenous Technological Change," *Journal of Political
     Economy*, vol. 98, no. 5 (October 1990): S71–S102 and "The Origins of Endogenous
     Growth," *Journal of Economic Perspectives*, vol. 8, no.1 (1994): 3–22; James Manyika,
     Daniel Pacthod, and Michael Park, "Translating Innovation Into U.S. Growth: An
     Advanced-Industries Perspective," McKinsey & Company, May 2011, http://mckinsey.
     com/industries/public-sector/our-insights/translating-innovation-into-us-growth-an-
     advanced-industries-perspective; James Manyika and Charles Roxburgh, "The Great
     Transformer: The Impact of the Internet on Economic Growth and Prosperity,"
     McKinsey Global Institute, October 2011.

3.   Commission on the Theft of American Intellectual Property, *The IP Commission Report*
     (Washington, DC: National Bureau of Asian Research, May 2013), http://
     ipcommission.org/report/IP_Commission_Report_052213.pdf.

4.   Klaus Schwab, "The Fourth Industrial Revolution," *Foreign Affairs*, December 12, 2015,
     http://foreignaffairs.com/articles/2015-12-12/fourth-industrial-revolution.

5. Richard Dobbs, James Manyika, and Jonathan Woetzel, *No Ordinary Disruption: The Four Global Forces Breaking All the Trends* (New York: Public Affairs, 2015).

6. Joe Andrews, "23andMe Competitor Veritas Genetics Slashes Price of Whole Genome Sequencing 40% to $600," CNBC, July 1, 2019, http://cnbc.com/2019/07/01/for-600-veritas-genetics-sequences-6point4-billion-letters-of-your-dna.html.

7. Edward Alden and Laura Taylor-Kale, *The Work Ahead: Machines, Skills, and U.S. Leadership in the Twenty-First Century* (New York: Council on Foreign Relations, 2018), http://cfr.org/report/the-work-ahead/report.

8. Carl Benedikt Frey and Michael A. Osborne, "The Future of Employment: How Susceptible Are Jobs to Computerization?," Oxford Martin School, September 1, 2013, https://www.oxfordmartin.ox.ac.uk/publications/the-future-of-employment; John Hawksworth, Richard Berriman, and Saloni Goel, "Will Robots Really Steal Our Jobs? An International Analysis of the Potential Long Term Impact of Automation," PwC, 2018, http://pwc.com/hu/hu/kiadvanyok/assets/pdf/impact_of_automation_on_jobs.pdf; Ljubica Nedelkoska and Glenda Quintini, "Automation, Skills Use and Training," OECD Social, Employment and Migration Working Papers no. 202 (Paris: OECD Publishing, 2018), http://doi.org/10.1787/2e2f4eea-en; James Manyika, Susan Lund, Michael Chui, Jacques Bughin, Jonathan Woetzel, Parul Batra, Ryan Ko, and Saurabh Sanghvi, "Jobs Lost, Jobs Gained: What the Future of Work Will Mean for Jobs, Skills, and Wages," McKinsey Global Institute, November 2017, http://mckinsey.com/featured-insights/future-of-work/jobs-lost-jobs-gained-what-the-future-of-work-will-mean-for-jobs-skills-and-wages.

9. Vannevar Bush, *Science: The Endless Frontier, A Report to the President* (Washington, DC: Director of the Office of Scientific Research and Development, July 1945), http://nsf.gov/od/lpa/nsf50/vbush1945.htm.

10. Mariana Mazzucato, *The Entrepreneurial State: Debunking Public vs. Private Sector Myths* (Anthem, 2013).

11. "National Defense Education and Innovation Initiative: Meeting America's Economic and Security Challenges in the 21st Century," Association of American Universities, January 2006, http://aau.edu/sites/default/files/AAU-Files/Key-Issues/Innovation-Competitiveness/Report-NDEII.pdf.

12. L. Fleming, H. Greene, G. Li, M. Marx, and D. Yao, "Government-Funded Research Increasingly Fuels Innovation," *Science* (June 21, 2019): 1139–1141.

13. Peter Singer, "Federally Supported Innovations," *Information Technology & Innovation Foundation*, February 3, 2015, http://itif.org/publications/2014/02/03/federally-supported-innovations; Harvard Business School, "Public Funding Essential for Advances in Biomedical Research: Cuts in National Institutes of Health Budget Could Impact Innovation," *ScienceDaily*, March 30, 2018, http://sciencedaily.com/releases/2017/03/170330142303.htm.

14. Simon Tripp and Martin Grueber, "Economic Impact of the Human Genome Project," Battelle Memorial Institute, May 2011, http://battelle.org/docs/default-source/misc/battelle-2011-misc-economic-impact-human-genome-project.pdf.

15. Center for American Entrepreneurship, "Immigrant Founders of the 2017 Fortune 500," http://startupsusa.org/fortune500.

16. David Ewalt, "Reuters Top 100: The World's Most Innovative Universities—2017," Reuters, September 27, 2017, http://reuters.com/article/us-amers-reuters-ranking-innovative-univ/reuters-top-100-the-worlds-most-innovative-universities-2017-idUSKCN1C209R.

17. J. John Wu, "Why U.S. Business R&D Is Not as Strong as It Appears," ITIF, June 2018, http://www2.itif.org/2018-us-business-rd.pdf.

18. Timothy Martin, "American Tech Firms Are Winning the R&D Spending Race With China," *Wall Street Journal*, October 30, 2018, http://wsj.com/articles/american-tech-firms-are-winning-the-r-d-spending-race-with-china-1540873318.

19. Pitchbook and National Venture Capital Association, *Venture Monitor* 4Q 2018, http://nvca.org/wp-content/uploads/delightful-downloads/2019/01/4Q_2018_PitchBook_NVCA_Venture_Monitor-1.pdf.

20. National Science Board, "Global Trends in Trade of Knowledge- and Technology-Intensive Products and Services," in *Science and Engineering Indicators 2018* (January 2018), http://nsf.gov/statistics/2018/nsb20181/report/sections/industry-technology-and-the-global-marketplace/global-trends-in-trade-of-knowledge--and-technology-intensive-products-and-services.

21. Mark Boroush, "U.S. R&D Increased by $20 Billion in 2015, to $495 Billion; Estimates for 2016 Indicate a Rise to $510 Billion," InfoBrief NSF 18-306, National Science Foundation, December 14, 2017, http://nsf.gov/statistics/2018/nsf18306.

22. "US R&D Spending at All-Time High, Federal Share Reaches Record Low," AIP, November 8, 2016, http://aip.org/fyi/2016/us-rd-spending-all-time-high-federal-share-reaches-record-low.

23. Jeffrey Mervis, "Data Check: U.S. Government Share of Basic Research Funding Falls Below 50%," *Science*, March 9, 2017, http://sciencemag.org/news/2017/03/data-check-us-government-share-basic-research-funding-falls-below-50.

24. Matt Hourihan and David Parkes, "Omnibus Would Provide Largest Research Increase in Nearly a Decade," AAAS, March 22, 2018, http://aaas.org/news/omnibus-would-provide-largest-research-increase-nearly-decade.

25. Joel Achenbach, Ben Guarino, Sarah Kaplan, and Brady Dennis, "Trump Budget Seeks Cuts in Science Funding," *Washington Post*, March 11, 2019, http://washingtonpost.com/science/2019/03/11/trump-budget-seeks-cuts-science-funding.

26. Robert Atkinson, Stephen Ezell, and John Wu, "Why Tariffs on Chinese ICT Imports Would Harm the U.S. Economy," ITIF, March 16, 2018, http://itif.org/publications/2018/03/16/why-tariffs-chinese-ict-imports-would-harm-us-economy.

27. Chad Brown and Eva Zhang, "Measuring Trump's 2018 Trade Protection: Five Takeaways," *Trade and Investment Policy Watch* (blog), PIIE, February 15, 2019, http://piie.com/blogs/trade-investment-policy-watch/measuring-trumps-2018-trade-protection-five-takeaways.

28. European Commission, "EU-China—A Strategic Outlook," June 12, 2019, http://ec.europa.eu/commission/sites/beta-political/files/communication-eu-china-a-strategic-outlook.pdf.

29. Edward Alden, "Trump and the TPP: Giving Away Something for Nothing," *Renewing*

America (blog), Council on Foreign Relations, January 23, 2017, http://cfr.org/blog/trump-and-tpp-giving-away-something-nothing.

30. Ehsan Masood, "How China Is Redrawing the Map of World Science," *Nature*, May 1, 2019, http://nature.com/immersive/d41586-019-01124-7/index.html.

31. Sari Pekkala Kerr, William Kerr, Çağlar Özden, and Christopher Parsons, *High-Skilled Migration and Agglomeration*, NBER Working Paper (December 2016), http://nber.org/papers/w22926; Michelle Hackman and Douglas Belkin, "Fewer International Students Heading to the U.S.," *Wall Street Journal*, November 13, 2018, http://wsj.com/articles/fewer-international-students-heading-to-the-u-s-1542105004.

32. "Travel Ban Throws Research, Academic Exchange Into Turmoil," CNBC, January 31, 2017, http://cnbc.com/2017/01/31/travel-ban-throws-research-academic-exchange-into-turmoil.html; Richard Chirgwin, "IETF Moves Meeting From USA to Canada to Dodge Trump Travel Ban," *Register*, July 16, 2017, http://theregister.co.uk/2017/07/16/trump_travel_ban_sees_ietf_move_meeting_from_usa_to_canada.

33. Issie Lapowsky, "Visa Rejections for Tech Workers Spike Under Trump," *Wired*, April 25, 2019, http://wired.com/story/h-1b-visa-rejections-spike-under-trump.

34. Rani Molla, "U.S. Companies Are Moving Tech Jobs to Canada Rather Than Deal With Trump's Immigration Policies," *Recode*, March 19, 2019, http://recode.net/2019/3/19/18264391/us-tech-jobs-canada-immigration-policies-trump.

35. Louise Radnofsky, "U.S. Changes Visa Process for High-Skilled Workers," *Wall Street Journal*, January 30, 2019.

36. Yi Xue and Richard C. Larson, "STEM Crisis or STEM Surplus? Yes and Yes," *Monthly Labor Review*, U.S. Bureau of Labor Statistics, May 2015, http://doi.org/10.21916/mlr.2015.14.

37. Xueying Han and Richard Applebaum, "Will They Stay or Will They Go? International STEM Students Are Up for Grabs," Kauffman Foundation, July 2016, http://kauffman.org/-/media/kauffman_org/research-reports-and-covers/2016/stem_students_final.pdf.

38. The STEM Imperative, Smithsonian Institution, http://ssec.si.edu/stem-imperative.

39. Celestine Bohlen, "Making Gains for Women in STEM Fields Will Take More Effort," *New York Times*, November 20, 2018, http://nytimes.com/2018/11/20/world/europe/women-in-stem.html.

40. Scott E. Page, *The Difference* (Princeton, NJ: Princeton University Press, 2007).

41. Donald Hicks, *Final Report of the Defense Science Board Task Force on Globalization and Security* (Washington, DC: Defense Science Board, 1999), ii.

42. Ben FitzGerald, Alexandra Sander, and Jacqueline Parziale, *Future Foundry: A New Strategic Approach to Military-Technical Advantage* (Washington, DC: CNAS, 2016), http://cnas.org/publications/reports/future-foundry.

43. "SASC Chairman John McCain Remarks on Top Defense Priorities for 114th Congress at CSIS," Senate Armed Services Committee, March 26, 2016, http://armed-services.senate.gov/press-releases/sasc-chairman-john-mccain-remarks-on-top-defense-priorities-for-114th-congress-at-csis.

44. *Summary of the 2018 National Defense Strategy of the United States* (Washington, DC: Department of Defense, 2018), http://dod.defense.gov/Portals/1/Documents/pubs/2018-National-Defense-Strategy-Summary.pdf.

45. J. Michael McQuade and Richard M. Murray, *Software Is Never Done: Refactoring the Acquisition Code for Competitive Advantage* (Defense Innovation Board, 2019), http://media.defense.gov/2019/apr/30/2002124828/-1/-1/0/softwareisneverdone_refactoringtheacquisitioncodeforcompetitiveadvantage_final.swap.report.pdf.

46. Jack Moore, "Here Are 10 of the Oldest IT Systems in the Federal Government," *Nextgov*, May 25, 2016, http://nextgov.com/cio-briefing/2016/05/10-oldest-it-systems-federal-government/128599.

47. Dennis Fisher, "Groundbreaking Cyber Fast Track Research Program Ending," *Threatpost*, March 6, 2016, http://threatpost.com/groundbreaking-cyber-fast-track-research-program-ending-030613/77594; Fred Kaplan, "The Pentagon's Innovation Experiment," *MIT Technology Review*, December 19, 2016, http://technologyreview.com/s/603084/the-pentagons-innovation-experiment.

48. Raj Shah, "Arceo's Shah on New Company, Defense Innovation, Tenure at DIUx," interview by Vago Muradian, *Defense and Aerospace Report*, December 28, 2018, http://youtube.com/watch?v=Ool1ctvS0h8; Mike Cerre, "How the Pentagon Joins Forces With Silicon Valley Startups," *PBS Newshour*, August 15, 2018, http://pbs.org/newshour/show/how-the-pentagon-joins-forces-with-silicon-valley-startups.

49. *Promoting DOD's Culture of Innovation: Statement Before the House Armed Services Committee,* 115th Cong. (2018) (statement of Dr. Eric Schmidt, Chairman, Defense Innovation Board, Department of Defense), http://docs.house.gov/meetings/AS/AS00/20180417/108132/HHRG-115-AS00-Wstate-SchmidtE-20180417.pdf.

50. Mark Wallace, "The U.S. Air Force Learned to Code—and Saved the Pentagon Millions," *Fast Company*, July 5, 2018, http://fastcompany.com/40588729/the-air-force-learned-to-code-and-saved-the-pentagon-millions.

51. Issie Lapowsky, "The Pentagon Is Building a Dream Team of Tech-Savvy Soldiers," *Wired*, July 2, 2018, http://wired.com/story/pentagon-dream-team-tech-savvy-soldiers.

52. Martin Martishak, "Defense Digital Service Chief Stepping Down After 'Nerd Tour of Duty,'" *Politico*, April 23, 2019, http://politico.com/story/2019/04/23/chris-lynch-leaving-defense-digital-1373893.

53. Ryan Mac, "Behind the Crash of 3D Robotics, North America's Most Promising Drone Company," *Forbes*, October 5, 2016, http://forbes.com/sites/ryanmac/2016/10/05/3d-robotics-solo-crash-chris-anderson.

54. National Defense Strategy Commission, *Providing for the Common Defense: The Assessment and Recommendations of the National Defense Strategy Commission* (Washington, DC: U.S. Institute of Peace, November 13, 2018), http://usip.org/sites/default/files/2018-11/providing-for-the-common-defense.pdf; Interagency Task Force in Fulfillment of Executive Order 13806, *Assessing and Strengthening the Manufacturing and Defense Industrial Base and Supply Chain Resiliency of the United States,* Report to President Donald J. Trump, September 2018, http://media.defense.gov/2018/oct/05/2002048904/-1/-1/1/assessing-and-strengthening-the-manufacturing-and%20defense-industrial-base-and-supply-chain-resiliency.pdf.

55. Adam Segal, *Rebuilding Trust Between Silicon Valley and Washington* (New York: Council on Foreign Relations, 2017), http://cfr.org/report/rebuilding-trust-between-silicon-valley-and-washington.

56. Scott Shane and Daisuke Wakabayashi, "Google Will Not Renew Pentagon Contract That Upset Employees," *New York Times*, June 1, 2018, http://nytimes.com/2018/06/01/technology/google-pentagon-project-maven.html.

57. Zachary Freyer Biggs, "Inside the Pentagon's Plans to Win Over Silicon Valley's AI Experts," *Wired*, December 21, 2018, http://wired.com/story/inside-the-pentagons-plan-to-win-over-silicon-valleys-ai-experts.

58. Joseph Bernstein, "Survey: 51% Of Tech Industry Workers Believe President Trump Has a Point About the Media Creating Fake News," BuzzFeed, February 23, 2019, http://buzzfeednews.com/article/josephbernstein/tech-industry-survey.

59. Heather Kelly, "Jeff Bezos: Amazon Will Keep Working With the DOD," CNN, October 15, 2018, http://cnn.com/2018/10/15/tech/jeff-bezos-wired/index.html.

60. John Sargent Jr., "Global Research and Development Expenditures: Fact Sheet," Congressional Research Service, June 27, 2018, http://fas.org/sgp/crs/misc/R44283.pdf; "Global R&D Continues Growth With Less Government Support," *R&D Magazine*, 2018, http://digital.rdmag.com/researchanddevelopment/2018_global_r_d_funding_forecast?pg=2#pg2.

61. OECD Data, "Gross Domestic Spending on R&D," last updated 2019, http://data.oecd.org/rd/gross-domestic-spending-on-r-d.htm.

62. Dennis Normille, "China Narrows U.S. Lead in R&D Spending," *Science*, October 19, 2018, http://science.sciencemag.org/content/362/6412/276; "The Rise of China in Science and Engineering: 2018," National Science Board, http://nsf.gov/nsb/sei/one-pagers/China-2018.pdf.

63. Normille, "China Narrows U.S. Lead in R&D Spending."

64. "China Now Produces Twice as Many Graduates a Year as the United States," World Economic Forum, April 13, 2017, http://weforum.org/agenda/2017/04/higher-education-in-china-has-boomed-in-the-last-decade; "Back to School Statistics," National Center for Education Statistics, http://nces.ed.gov/fastfacts/display.asp?id=372.

65. Richard P. Appelbaum and Xueying Han, "China's Science, Technology, Engineering, and Mathematics (STEM) Research Environment: A Snapshot," *PLOS One*, April 3, 2018, https://doi.org/10.1371/journal.pone.0195347.

66. National Science Board, "International S&E Higher Education," in *Science & Engineering Indicators 2018*, http://nsf.gov/statistics/2018/nsb20181/report/sections/higher-education-in-science-and-engineering/international-s-e-higher-education.

67. Dennis Normille, "With Generous Funding and Top-Tier Jobs, China Seeks to Lure Science Talent From Abroad," *Science*, June 5, 2018, http://sciencemag.org/news/2018/06/generous-funding-and-top-tier-jobs-china-seeks-lure-science-talent-abroad.

68. Hepeng Jia, "China's Plan to Recruit Talented Researchers," *Nature*, January 17, 2018, http://nature.com/articles/d41586-018-00538-z.

69. Kate O'Keeffe and Timothy Puko, "U.S. Targets Efforts by China, Others to Recruit Government Scientists," *Wall Street Journal*, June 10, 2019, http://wsj.com/articles/energy-department-bans-personnel-from-foreign-talent-recruitment-programs-11560182546.

70. "Hyperion: China Maintains Lead in Race to Exascale," *HPC Wire*, June 28, 2018, http://hpcwire.com/2018/06/28/hyperion-china-maintains-lead-in-race-to-exascale. It is worth noting that the United States still excels in terms of supercomputing software, which is critical to harnessing the power of supercomputers for useful applications.

71. Shannon Ellis, "Biotech Booms in China," *Nature*, January 17, 2018, http://nature.com/articles/d41586-018-00542-3.

72. Peng Ying, "AI Sector Sees Big Investment, Financing in 2017: Report," *Xinhua*, February 24, 2018, http://xinhuanet.com/english/2018-02/24/c_136997279.htm.

73. Yujia He, "How China Is Preparing for an AI-Powered Future," Wilson Center, June 2017, http://wilsoncenter.org/sites/default/files/how_china_is_preparing_for_ai_powered_future.pdf.

74. Yoav Shoham, Raymond Perrault, Erik Brynjolfsson, Jack Clark, James Manyika, Juan Carlos Niebles, Terah Lyons, John Etchemendy, Barbara Grosz and Zoe Bauer, *AI Index 2018 Annual Report* (Stanford, CA: Stanford University, December 2018), http://cdn.aiindex.org/2018/AI%20Index%202018%20Annual%20Report.pdf; Jun Zhu, Tiejun Huang, Wenguang Chen, and Wen Gao, "The Future of Artificial Intelligence in China," *Communications of the ACM 61*, no. 11 (November 2018): 44–45.

75. He, "How China Is Preparing for an AI-Powered Future"; Chen Xi, "China to Open 400 Big Data, AI Majors in Universities for Global Competition," *Global Times*, February 27, 2019.

76. Will Knight, "China's Huawei Has Big Ambitions to Weaken the U.S. Grip on AI Leadership," *Technology Review*, March 4, 2019, http://technologyreview.com/s/612914/chinas-huawei-has-big-ambitions-to-weaken-the-uss-grip-on-ai-leadership.

77. Jason Rowley, "Q4 2018 Closes Out a Record Year for the Global VC Market," *Crunchbase News*, January 7, 2019, http://news.crunchbase.com/news/q4-2018-closes-out-a-record-year-for-the-global-vc-market.

78. Lorand Laskai, "In Drive for Tech Independence, Xi Doubles Down on Civil-Military Fusion," *China Brief*, May 9, 2018, http://jamestown.org/program/in-drive-for-tech-independence-xi-doubles-down-on-civil-military-fusion.

79. Adam Segal, "When China Rules the Web," *Foreign Affairs*, September/October 2018.

80. National Science Board, "Gross Expenditure on R&D for Selected Countries, by Performing Sector or Source of Funds: 2015 or Most Recent Year," in *Science and Engineering Indicators 2018* (January 2018), accessed July 9, 2019, http://nsf.gov/statistics/2018/nsb20181/data/tables.

81. Adam Segal, "Seizing Core Technologies: China Responds to U.S. Technology Competition," *China Leadership Monitor*, June 1, 2019, http://prcleader.org/segal-clm-60.

82. White House, Presidential Executive Order on Streamlining and Expediting Requests to Locate Broadband Facilities in Rural America, January 8, 2018, http://whitehouse. gov/presidential-actions/presidential-executive-order-streamlining-expediting-requests-locate-broadband-facilities-rural-america; Committee on STEM Education of the National Science & Technology Council, *Charting a Course for Success: America's Strategy for STEM Education* (December 2018), http://whitehouse.gov/wp-content/uploads/2018/12/STEM-Education-Strategic-Plan-2018.pdf.

83. "FY19 Budget Request: Defense S&T Stable as DOD Focuses on Technology Transition," American Institute of Physics, February 23, 2018, http://aip.org/fyi/2018/fy19-budget-request-defense-st-stable-dod-focuses-technology-transition.

84. "FY2019 Department of Defense Appropriations," Association of American Universities, September 28, 2018, http://aau.edu/sites/default/files/AAU-Files/Key-Issues/Federal-Budget/Appropriations-Tables/Defense-FY19-Funding-Table.pdf; "Budget," Defense Advanced Research Projects Agency, accessed July 9, 2019, http://darpa.mil/about-us/budget.

85. Lauren C. Williams, "DIUx Gets a Big Boost in FY19 Budget," FCW, February 12, 2018, http://fcw.com/articles/2018/02/12/budget-williams-do.aspx; Jonathan Behrens, "FY20 Budget Request: DOD Science and Technology," American Institute of Physics, March 28, 2019.

86. Stephen Rodriguez and Evanna Hu, "America Needs an AI Strategy. Just Ask Google," *National Review*, July 18, 2018, http://nationalreview.com/2018/07/america-needs-an-ai-strategy-to-remain-global-technology-powerhouse.

87. Sydney Freedberg Jr., "Joint Artificial Intelligence Center Created Under DoD CIO," *Breaking Defense*, June 29, 2018, http://breakingdefense.com/2018/06/joint-artificial-intelligence-center-created-under-dod-cio.

88. White House, FY 2020 Administration Research and Development Budget Priorities, July 31, 2018, http://whitehouse.gov/wp-content/uploads/2018/07/M-18-22.pdf; Defense Advanced Research Projects Agency, AI Next Campaign, http://darpa.mil/work-with-us/ai-next-campaign.

89. White House Office of Science and Technology Policy, "Summary of the 2018 White House Summit on Artificial Intelligence for American Industry," May 10, 2018, http://whitehouse.gov/wp-content/uploads/2018/05/Summary-Report-of-White-House-AI-Summit.pdf.

90. White House, "Accelerating America's Leadership in Artificial Intelligence," February 11, 2019, http://whitehouse.gov/articles/accelerating-americas-leadership-in-artificial-intelligence.

91. U.S. Department of Defense, "Summary of the 2018 Department of Defense Artificial Intelligence Strategy," February 12, 2019, http://media.defense.gov/2019/feb/12/2002088963/-1/-1/1/summary-of-dod-ai-strategy.pdf.

92. Megan Lamberth, "The White House and Defense Department Unveiled AI Strategies. Now What?" C4ISRNet, February 27, 2019, http://c4isrnet.com/opinion/2019/02/27/the-white-house-and-defense-department-unveiled-ai-strategies-now-what.

93. White House, Presidential Memorandum on Developing a Sustainable Spectrum Strategy for America's Future, October 25, 2018, http://whitehouse.gov/presidential-

actions/presidential-memorandum-developing-sustainable-spectrum-strategy-americas-future.

94. Brian Fung, "5G Is About to Get a Big Boost From Trump and the FCC," *Washington Post*, April 12, 2019, http://washingtonpost.com/technology/2019/04/12/g-is-about-get-big-boost-trump-fcc.

95. Dan Strumpf, "Huawei Expects $30 Billion Revenue Hit From U.S. Clampdown," *Wall Street Journal*, June 17, 2019, http://wsj.com/articles/u-s-clampdown-to-cost-huawei-30-billion-in-revenue-founder-says-11560766359.

96. Peter Baker and Keith Bradsher, "Trump and Xi Agree to Restart Trade Talks, Avoiding Escalation in Tariff War," *New York Times*, June 29, 2019, http://nytimes.com/2019/06/29/world/asia/g20-trump-xi-trade-talks.html; "White House Official: New Sales to China's Huawei to Cover Only Widely Available Goods," Reuters, June 30, 2019, http://uk.reuters.com/article/us-usa-trade-china-huawei-tech/white-house-official-new-sales-to-chinas-huawei-to-cover-only-widely-available-goods-idUKKCN1TV0PO.

97. Julian Barnes and Adam Satariano, "U.S. Campaign to Ban Huawei Overseas Stumbles as Allies Resist," *New York Times*, March 17, 2019, http://nytimes.com/2019/03/17/us/politics/huawei-ban.html.

98. Marco Rubio (@marcorubio), "If President Trump has agreed to reverse recent sanctions against #Huawei he has made a catastrophic mistake . . . ," Twitter, June 29, 2019, 7:34 a.m., http://twitter.com/marcorubio/status/1144977483101593601.

99. Rhodium Group and National Committee on U.S.-China Relations, "Two Way Street: 2019 Update U.S.-China Investment Trends," May 7, 2019, http://arraysproduction-0dot22.s3.amazonaws.com/rhodiumgroup/assets/icon/RHG_TWS-2019_Executive-Summary_7May2019.pdf.

100. Brian Gormley, "Startups Rethink Foreign Funding as U.S. Tightens Security Reviews," *Wall Street Journal*, March 15, 2019, http://wsj.com/articles/startups-rethink-foreign-funding-as-u-s-tightens-security-reviews-11552649400.

101. Rolfe Winkler, "Chinese Cash That Powered Silicon Valley Is Suddenly Toxic," *Wall Street Journal*, June 11, 2019, http://wsj.com/articles/chinese-cash-is-suddenly-toxic-in-silicon-valley-following-u-s-pressure-campaign-11560263302.

102. Christina Farr and Ari Levy, "The Trump Administration Is Forcing This Health Start-Up That Took Chinese Money Into a Fire Sale," CNBC, April 4, 2019, http://cnbc.com/2019/04/04/cfius-forces-patientslikeme-into-fire-sale-booting-chinese-investor.html.

103. Heather Somerville, "Chinese Tech Investors Flee Silicon Valley as Trump Tightens Scrutiny," Reuters, http://reuters.com/article/us-venture-china-regulation-insight/chinese-tech-investors-flee-silicon-valley-as-trump-tightens-scrutiny-idUSKCN1P10CB.

104. "A Conversation With Christopher Wray," Council on Foreign Relations, April 26, 2019, http://cfr.org/event/conversation-christopher-wray-0.

105. Elizabeth Redden, "Science vs. Security," *Inside Higher Ed*, April 16, 2019, http://insidehighered.com/news/2019/04/16/federal-granting-agencies-and-lawmakers-step-scrutiny-foreign-research.

106. Patricia Zengerle and Matt Spetalnick, "Exclusive: Fearing Espionage, U.S. Weighs Tighter Rules on Chinese Students," Reuters, November 29, 2018, http://reuters.com/article/us-usa-china-students-exclusive/exclusive-fearing-espionage-us-weighs-tighter-rules-on-chinese-students-idUSKCN1NY1HE.

107. Jenny Leonard and David McLaughlin, "U.S. Presses Ahead on Plan to Limit High-Tech Exports," *Bloomberg*, December 11, 2018, http://bloomberg.com/news/articles/2018-12-11/u-s-plan-to-limit-high-tech-exports-forges-on-amid-trade-truce.

108. Ana Swanson, Paul Mozur, and Steve Lohr, "U.S. Blacklists More Chinese Tech Companies Over National Security Concerns," *New York Times*, June 21, 2019, http://nytimes.com/2019/06/21/us/politics/us-china-trade-blacklist.html.

109. Jack Stubbs, Joseph Menn, and Chris Bing, "Inside the West's Failed Fight Against China's 'Cloud Hopper' Hackers," Reuters, June 26, 2019, http://reuters.com/investigates/special-report/china-cyber-cloudhopper.

110. "Attorney General Jeff Sessions Announces New Initiative to Combat Chinese Economic Espionage," U.S. Department of Justice, November 1, 2018, http://justice.gov/opa/speech/attorney-general-jeff-sessions-announces-new-initiative-combat-chinese-economic-espionage.

111. Department of Justice, "Chinese Intelligence Officers and Their Recruited Hackers and Insiders Conspired to Steal Sensitive Commercial Aviation and Technological Data for Years," press release, October 30, 2019, http://justice.gov/opa/pr/chinese-intelligence-officers-and-their-recruited-hackers-and-insiders-conspired-steal; "Deputy Attorney General Rod J. Rosenstein Announces Charges Against Chinese Hackers," Department of Justice, December 20, 2018, http://justice.gov/opa/speech/deputy-attorney-general-rod-j-rosenstein-announces-charges-against-chinese-hackers; Department of Justice, "PRC State-Owned Company, Taiwan Company, and Three Individuals Charged With Economic Espionage," press release, November 1, 2018, http://justice.gov/opa/pr/prc-state-owned-company-taiwan-company-and-three-individuals-charged-economic-espionage.

112. "Innovation Nation: An American Innovation Agenda for 2020," Business Roundtable, January 2019, http://s3.amazonaws.com/brt.org/BRT_Innovation_report_pages_00l.pdf.

113. Kenneth Flamm and Qifei Wang, "SEMATECH Revisited: Assessing Consortium Impacts on Semiconductor Industry R&D," in *Securing the Future: Regional and National Programs to Support the Semiconductor Industry*, ed. Charles W. Wessner (Washington, DC: National Academies Press, 2003).

114. Joshua New, "Why the United States Needs a National Artificial Intelligence Strategy and What It Should Look Like," Center for Data Innovation, December 4, 2018, http://www2.datainnovation.org/2018-national-ai-strategy.pdf.

115. New, "Why the United States Needs a National Artificial Intelligence Strategy."

116. OPEN Government Data Act of 2016, S.2852, 114th Cong. (2016), http://congress.gov/bill/114th-congress/senate-bill/2852.

117. Julia Angwin and Jeff Larson, "Bias in Criminal Risk Scores Is Mathematically Inevitable, Researchers Say," *ProPublica*, December 30, 2016, http://propublica.org/article/bias-in-criminal-risk-scores-is-mathematically-inevitable-researchers-say.

118. "Ensuring Long-Term U.S. Leadership in Semiconductors," President's Council of Advisors on Science and Technology, January 2017, http://obamawhitehouse.archives. gov/sites/default/files/microsites/ostp/PCAST/pcast_ensuring_long-term_us_ leadership_in_semiconductors.pdf.

119. Milo Medin and Gilman Louie, "The 5G Ecosystem: Risks & Opportunities for DoD," Defense Innovation Board, April 3, 2019, http://media.defense.gov/2019/ Apr/04/2002109654/-1/-1/0/DIB_5G_STUDY_04.04.19.PDF.

120. Jeremy Hsu, "How the U.S. Can Prepare to Live in China's 5G World," IEEE Spectrum, April 23, 2019, http://spectrum.ieee.org/tech-talk/telecom/standards/ how-america-can-prepare-to-live-in-chinas-5g-world.

121. Louise Lucas, "Huawei Revenue Rises 39% Despite US Pressure on 5G," *Financial Times*, April 22, 2019, http://ft.com/content/2cdd5dec-64b6-11e9-9adc-98bf1d35a056.

122. Medin and Louie, "The 5G Ecosystem: Risks & Opportunities for DoD."

123. Kiran Stacey, "Why Is There No US Rival to Compete With Huawei?" *Financial Times*, April 26, 2019, http://ft.com/content/18d3823a-65f2-11e9-9adc-98bf1d35a056.

124. Nicol Turner Lee, "Will the US Be 5G Ready?," *TechTank* (blog), Brookings Institution, July 13, 2018, http://brookings.edu/blog/techtank/2018/07/13/will-the-us-be-5g-ready.

125. *Hearing on 5G: The Impact on National Security, Intellectual Property, and Competition: Statement Before the Senate Committee on the Judiciary*, 116th Cong. (2019) (statement of Dr. Charles Clancy, Bradley Professor of Cybersecurity, Virginia Tech), http:// judiciary.senate.gov/imo/media/doc/Clancy%20Testimony.pdf.

126. Ryan McMorrow, "Huawei a Key Beneficiary of China Subsidies That US Wants Ended," Phys.org, May 30, 2019, http://phys.org/news/2019-05-huawei-key-beneficiary-china-subsidies.html.

127. Lenka Ponilkeska, "Countries Seek United 5G Security Approach Amid Huawei Concerns," *Bloomberg*, May 3, 2019, http://bloomberg.com/news/articles/2019-05-03/ countries-seek-united-5g-security-approach-amid-huawei-concerns.

128. Stephen Castle, "Pompeo Attacks China and Warns Britain Over Huawei Security Risks," *New York Times*, May 8, 2019, http://nytimes.com/2019/05/08/technology/ pompeo-huawei-britain.html.

129. Medin and Louie, "The 5G Ecosystem: Risks & Opportunities for DoD."

130. *Times Higher Education*, "World University Rankings 2019 by Subject: Engineering and Technology," http://timeshighereducation.com/world-university-rankings/2019/ subject-ranking/engineering-and-IT#!/page/0/length/25/sort_by/rank/sort_order/asc/ cols/stats.

131. Jeff Stone, "Corporate Giants Want to Help Students, Feds and Themselves by Offering Cyber Pros $75,000 in Loan Assistance," *Cyberscoop*, April 10, 2019, http:// cyberscoop.com/workforce-cyber-talent-initiative-loan-assistance.

132. Yangyang Cheng, "Don't Close the Door on Chinese Scientists Like Me," *Foreign Policy*, June 4, 2018, http://foreignpolicy.com/2018/06/04/dont-close-the-door-on-chinese-scientists-like-me.

133. "National Policy on the Transfer of Scientific, Technical, and Engineering Information," National Security Decision Directives (Federation of American Scientists, September 21, 1985), http://fas.org/irp/offdocs/nsdd/nsdd-189.htm.

134. Secretary of the Air Force Public Affairs, "$40M Available for Start-Ups, Small Businesses Through Air Force Pitch Day," Air Force Materiel Command, January 15, 2019,http://afmc.af.mil/News/Article-Display/Article/1732301/40m-available-for-start-ups-small-businesses-through-air-force-pitch-day.

135. "Mobilizing Tech Talent," Partnership for Public Service, September 18, 2018, http://ourpublicservice.org/wp-content/uploads/2018/09/Mobilizing_Tech_Talent-2018.09.26.pdf.

136. Mark Hagerott and James Stravridis, "Trump's Big Defense Buildup Should Include a National Cyber Academy," *Foreign Policy*, March 21, 2017, http://foreignpolicy.com/2017/03/21/trumps-big-defense-buildup-should-include-a-national-cyber-academy-military-education.

137. Amy Zegart and Kevin Childs, "The Divide Between Silicon Valley and Washington Is a National-Security Threat," *Atlantic*, December 13, 2018, http://theatlantic.com/ideas/archive/2018/12/growing-gulf-between-silicon-valley-and-washington/577963.

138. Exec. Order No. 13875, 84, C.F.R. 28711 (2019), http://whitehouse.gov/presidential-actions/executive-order-evaluating-improving-utility-federal-advisory-committees.

139. Joel Meyer, "Startups Should Love Government Work," *Defense One*, February 8, 2019, http://defenseone.com/ideas/2019/02/startups-should-love-government-work/154722/?oref=d-channeltop.

140. Stephen Ezell and Caleb Foote, "How Stringent Export Controls on Emerging Technologies Would Harm the U.S. Economy," Information Technology and Innovation Foundation, May 20, 2019, http://itif.org/publications/2019/05/20/how-stringent-export-controls-emerging-technologies-would-harm-us-economy.

141. Cade Metz, "Curbs on A.I. Exports? Silicon Valley Fears Losing Its Edge," *New York Times*, January 1, 2019, http://nytimes.com/2019/01/01/technology/artificial-intelligence-export-restrictions.html.

142. A Bill to Establish the Office of Critical Technologies and Security, and for Other Purposes, S.29, 116th Cong. (2019), http://congress.gov/bill/116th-congress/senate-bill/29.

143. Securing American Science and Technology Act of 2019, H.R. 3038, 116th Cong. (2019), https://www.congress.gov/116/bills/hr3038/BILLS-116hr3038ih.pdf.

144. James Manyika, Susan Lund, Marc Singer, Olivia White, and Chris Berry, "How Digital Finance Could Boost Growth in Emerging Economies," McKinsey Global Institute, September 2016, http://mckinsey.com/featured-insights/employment-and-growth/how-digital-finance-could-boost-growth-in-emerging-economies.

145. Nigel Cory, "Cross-Border Data Flows: Where Are the Barriers, and What Do They Cost?," Information Technology and Innovation Foundation, May 1, 2017, http://itif.org/publications/2017/05/01/cross-border-data-flows-where-are-barriers-and-what-do-they-cost.

146. Samm Sacks and Manyi Kathy Li, "How Chinese Cybersecurity Standards Impact

Doing Business in China," Center for Strategic and International Studies, August 2, 2018, http://csis.org/analysis/how-chinese-cybersecurity-standards-impact-doing-business-china.

147. Hilary McGeachy, "U.S.-China Technology Competition: Impacting a Rules-Based Order," May 2, 2019, United States Studies Centre, University of Sydney, http://ussc.edu.au/analysis/us-china-technology-competition-impacting-a-rules-based-order.

148. Lee G. Branstetter, Britta Glennon, and J. Bradford Jensen, "The Rise of Global Innovation by US Multinationals Poses Risks and Opportunities," Peterson Institute for International Economics, June 2019, http://piie.com/research/piie-charts/us-multinational-corporations-have-shifted-foreign-rd-towards-nontraditional.

149. *International Science and Technology Cooperation: Statement Before the Subcomm. on Research and Science Education*, 110th Cong. (2008) (statement of Dr. Nina V. Federoff, Science and Technology Advisor to the Secretary of State).

150. Daniel Kliman and Brendan Thomas Noone, "How the Five Eyes Can Harness Commercial Innovation," *DefenseOne*, June 25, 2018, http://defenseone.com/ideas/2018/07/how-five-eyes-can-harness-commercial-innovation/150040.

151. U.S. Department of Energy, 75 *Breakthroughs by the U.S. Department of Energy's National Laboratories* (Livermore, CA: Lawrence Livermore National Laboratory Public Affairs Office, 2017), http://energy.gov/downloads/75-breakthroughs-americas-national-laboratories.

152. Philip Rossetti, "Publicly Funded National Labs Important to U.S. Innovation," American Action Forum, February 14, 2018, http://americanactionforum.org/research/publicly-funded-national-labs-still-important-u-s-innovation.

153. Task Force on U.S.-China Policy, Orville Schell and Susan L. Shirk, ed., *Course Correction: Toward an Effective and Sustainable China Policy.*

ACRONYMS

AI
artificial intelligence

BRI
Belt and Road Initiative

CFIUS
Committee on Foreign
Investment in the United States

CPTPP
Comprehensive and Progressive
Agreement for Trans-Pacific
Partnership

DARPA
Defense Advanced Research
Projects Agency

DDS
Defense Digital Service

DHS
Department of
Homeland Security

DIB
Defense Innovation Board

DIU
Defense Innovation Unit

DOD
Department of Defense

DOE
Department of Energy

DREAM Act
Development, Relief, and
Education for Alien Minors Act

FCC
Federal Communications
Commission

FIRRMA
Foreign Investment Risk Review
Modernization Act

GDP
gross domestic product

GPS
Global Positioning System

ICT
information and
communications technology

IP
intellectual property

JAIC
Joint Artificial Intelligence
Center

NDAA
National Defense
Authorization Act

NDEA
National Defense Education Act

NIH
National Institutes of Health

NIST
National Institute of Standards
and Technology

NSS
National Security Strategy

NSF
National Science Foundation

OAI
Office of American Innovation

OECD
Organization for Economic
Cooperation and Development

OSTP
Office of Science and
Technology Policy

R&D
research and development

STEM
science, technology, engineering,
and mathematics

VC
venture capital

WTO
World Trade Organization

GLOSSARY

additive printing
The manufacturing of solid, three-dimensional objects by adding together layers of material (such as plastic); also known as 3-D printing.

artificial intelligence (AI)
A branch of computer science dealing with the simulation of intelligent behavior in computers.

basic research
The systematic study of the fundamental aspects of phenomena and observable facts, without specific applications toward processes or products.

biotechnology
Technology that harnesses biological systems or living organisms to solve problems and develop products.

Committee on Foreign Investment in the United States
A federal interagency committee authorized to review certain transactions involving foreign investment in the United States to determine the effects of such transactions on U.S. national security.

cybersecurity
The prevention of damage to, unauthorized use of, and exploitation of electronic information and communications systems, and their restoration when compromised, in order to strengthen the confidentiality, integrity, and availability of these systems.

encryption
The transformation of data (called "plaintext") into a form (called "ciphertext") that conceals the data's original meaning to prevent it from being understood or used.

exascale supercomputer
A computer with an operating speed of one quintillion (one billion billion) calculations per second. Such a computer can analyze massive volumes of data quickly and realistically model and simulate complex processes.

5G
Fifth-generation cellular networks. The term is also used as shorthand for the technologies involved in the workings of such a network, including the radio frequencies used and the ways in which components, such as computer chips and antennae, handle radio signals and exchange data.

genomics
Comprehensive methods for studying the molecular biology of genes, cells, and physiology.

H-1B visa
An employment-based visa that allows U.S. employers to temporarily employ foreign workers in specialty occupations or in research and development projects administered by the U.S. Department of Defense.

hydraulic fracturing (fracking)
Injection of a fluid at high pressure into an underground rock formation to open fissures and allow trapped gas or crude oil to flow through a pipe to a wellhead at the surface.

information technology (IT)
The development, maintenance, study, and use of computer systems, software, and networks for the storing, processing, and distribution of data.

intellectual property (IP)
Creations of the mind such as musical, literary, and artistic works; inventions; and symbols, names, images, and designs used in commerce, including copyrights, trademarks, and patents. Under intellectual property law, the holder of one of these abstract "properties" has certain exclusive rights to it.

legacy system
A computer system, programming language, software application, or other technology that is outdated or can no longer receive support and maintenance but is essential for organizations or companies and cannot easily be replaced or updated.

moonshot
An ambitious, exploratory, and potentially groundbreaking project undertaken with high risk and without expectation of immediate profitability or benefit. The term is derived from the U.S. Apollo 11 spaceflight mission.

open-source technology
Technology in which the source code is made publicly available, which allows for its modification and free redistribution. This is in contrast to closed-source or proprietary practices, in which the source code is secret.

quantum information
A field of science and technology that draws from the disciplines of physical science, mathematics, computer science, and engineering. The field's aim is to determine how fundamental laws of physics can be harnessed to dramatically improve the acquisition, transmission, and processing of information.

robotics
An engineering discipline dealing with the design, construction, and operation of any automatically operated machine that replaces human effort. The machine need not resemble human beings in appearance or perform functions in a humanlike manner.

seed-stage funding
The initial capital invested in the early development of a business or product, and the first of four official equity funding stages for start-ups.

seismic imaging
The process of directing an intense sound underground and recording the sound waves as they echo within the earth. Data processing then turns the recordings into images of geologic structures, with the goal of evaluating conditions underground.

semiconductor
Any of a class of crystalline solids that in terms of electrical conductivity are intermediate between a conductor and an insulator. Semiconductors are used in manufacturing various kinds of electronic devices, including diodes, transistors, and integrated circuits.

Series A investment
Funding in a privately held start-up company after it has shown progress in building its business model and demonstrated the potential to grow and generate revenue. This follows the initial seed-stage funding and precedes Series B and C investments.

spectrum
The entire distribution of electromagnetic radiation, ordered according to frequency or wavelength. The spectrum includes several distinct portions, based on differences in behavior in the waves' emission, transmission, and absorption and their practical applications. In wireless technology, spectrum refers to the radio portion of the electromagnetic spectrum, ranging from low-band (frequency of less than one gigahertz) to high-band (twenty-four to fifty gigahertz). Mid-band spectrum is typically one to six gigahertz.

Sputnik
Any of a series of ten artificial Earth satellites that the Soviet Union launched starting on October 4, 1957, inaugurating the space age.

Sputnik 1, the first human-launched satellite, was seen as a tipping point in the Space Race, the technological competition between the United States and Soviet Union that constituted part of the Cold War.

synthetic biology
A field of research in which the main objective is to create fully operational biological systems from the smallest constituent parts possible, including DNA, proteins, and other organic molecules.

techno-nationalism
The practice of asserting national strength through technological supremacy and investment in industries of the future.

venture capital
Financing that investors provide to start-up companies and small businesses that are believed to have long-term growth potential. Funding is done in rounds, potentially with multiple investors.

TASK FORCE MEMBERS

Task Force members are asked to join a consensus signifying that they endorse "the general policy thrust and judgments reached by the group, though not necessarily every finding and recommendation." They participate in the Task Force in their individual, not their institutional, capacities.

Alana Ackerson is cofounder and chief people officer at Figure, where the primary mission is to build and promote self-sufficient, independent blockchain solutions to eliminate rent-seeking and facilitate innovation in financial services. Ackerson also held the position of chief executive officer of the Thiel Foundation, where she led the organization's efforts to support the next generation of entrepreneurs and promote radical scientific and technological innovations. Previously, she served as partner and president of Cabezon Investment Group and vice president of SoFi. Ackerson holds a BA in science, technology, and society from Stanford University, an MA in philosophical and systematic theology from the Graduate Theological Union, Berkeley, and a doctorate of ministry with a focus on technology and faith from San Francisco Theological Seminary.

Doug Beck is vice president, Americas and Northeast Asia, for Apple. Previously, he was based in Tokyo and led Apple's businesses in northeast Asia. Beck joined Apple in 2009 from Charles Schwab, where he was senior vice president and chief strategy officer. Before Schwab, he was a partner at McKinsey & Company. Beck is an officer in the U.S. Navy Reserve and served from 2006 through 2007 in Iraq and Afghanistan with a joint special operations task force. He was awarded the Bronze Star Medal, Combat Action Ribbon, and Presidential Unit

Citation. He currently leads the joint reserve component of the Defense Innovation Unit. As a civilian, Beck serves as an executive advisor to the chief of naval operations and special operations community leadership and as an informal advisor to senior Defense Department leaders. Beck is a member of the boards of directors of the Center for a New American Security and Association of American Rhodes Scholars, and of the board of advisors of Yale University's Jackson Institute for Global Affairs. He holds a BA from Yale and an MPhil in international relations from Oxford University, where he was a Rhodes scholar.

Nicholas F. Beim is a partner at Venrock, a venture capital firm, where he focuses on artificial intelligence, software, and financial technology investments. His investments include Dataminr, a real-time AI platform that identifies critical breaking information from publicly available data sets; Percipient.ai, an advanced computer vision and machine learning analytics platform for national and corporate security; and Chisel.ai, an enterprise platform for a new class of intelligent insurance applications. Beim works actively with In-Q-Tel, the Defense Innovation Unit, and DARPA to accelerate innovation in the national security area. He also serves on the board of Endeavor, a nonprofit organization that supports high-growth entrepreneurs in emerging market countries, and on the advisory board of Columbia University's Center on Global Energy Policy.

Jim Breyer is the founder and CEO of Breyer Capital, a venture capital firm based in Menlo Park, California. Breyer has been an early investor in over forty technology companies that have completed successful public offerings or mergers. Many of these investments returned over one hundred times their cost, and more than a dozen returned over twenty-five times their cost. Breyer is also the co-chairman of IDG Capital, based in Beijing, with offices in Guangzhou, Hangzhou, Hong Kong, and Shanghai. He serves on the board of directors of Blackstone and previously served as an investor or lead director at Dell, Etsy, Facebook, Marvel Entertainment, 21st Century Fox, Walmart, and many other successful technology and media companies. He is also the chairman of the advisory board of Tsinghua University's School of Economics and Management. He is a fellow of the Harvard Corporation, Harvard University's senior governing board. Breyer is also a volunteer and board member at several philanthropic organizations, including Stanford University's Institute for Human-Centered Artificial Intelligence, of which he is a founding member.

Steven A. Denning is the chairman of General Atlantic (GA), which he has helped build into a leading global growth equity firm with over $30 billion in capital under management and fourteen offices worldwide. Denning joined GA in 1980 after working with McKinsey & Company. He previously served for six years in the U.S. Navy before attending business school. Denning serves on many boards, including at the Bridgespan Group, Council on Foreign Relations, Markle Foundation, Blue Meridian Partners, National Park Foundation, College Advising Corps, and Carnegie Endowment for International Peace. At Stanford University, he is chair of the Global Advisory Council to the President, advisory council of the Freeman Spogli Institute, and Natural Capital Advisory Council; he is also a member of Stanford's Knight-Hennessy Scholar Program advisory board and the advisory councils of the Stanford Distinguished Careers Institute and Institute for Human-Centered Artificial Intelligence. He is the former chair of Stanford's board of trustees and the advisory council at the Stanford Graduate School of Business. He is a director of Engility Corporation. Denning holds a BS from the Georgia Institute of Technology, an MS from the Naval Postgraduate School, and an MBA from the Stanford Graduate School of Business.

Regina E. Dugan is an internationally recognized business executive. She has led world-class global teams and hundred-million- to multibillion-dollar efforts to deliver breakthrough products at Facebook, Google, Motorola, and DARPA. She was the nineteenth director of DARPA, and the first woman director. Dugan has been described by *Fortune* as one of the world's leading experts on product innovation. She has been named to the Verge 50 list, *Fast Company*'s Most Creative People in Business 1000, the CNN 10: Thinkers, and CNBC's Next List. Dugan is coauthor of the *Harvard Business Review* (HBR) cover article "'Special Forces' Innovation: How DARPA Attacks Problems" and was a 2013 HBR McKinsey Award finalist. She has spoken at events including the Code Conferences D9 and D11, the *Washington Post* summit on U.S. competitiveness, and TED, where her 2012 talk was one of the top ten trending Twitter topics worldwide. She holds a BS/MS from Virginia Tech, where she was inducted to the Academy of Engineering Excellence, and a PhD from the California Institute of Technology.

Reid Hoffman is a partner at Greylock Partners and an accomplished entrepreneur, executive, and investor. He joined Greylock in 2009 from LinkedIn, which he cofounded in 2003. He serves on the boards of Airbnb, Apollo Fusion, Aurora, Coda, Convoy, Entrepreneur First, Gixo, Microsoft, Nauto, Xapo, and several early-stage companies. Hoffman also serves on a number of nonprofit boards, including at Kiva, Endeavor, CZI Biohub, Do Something, Stanford's Institute for Human-Centered Artificial Intelligence, and the MacArthur Foundation's 100&Change. He is the host of the podcast *Masters of Scale*, the first American media program to commit to a fifty-fifty gender balance for featured guests. Hoffman is the coauthor of two *New York Times* best-selling books, *The Start-Up of You: Adapt to the Future, Invest in Yourself, and Transform Your Career* and *The Alliance: Managing Talent in the Networked Age*. His newest book is *Blitzscaling: The Lightning-Fast Path to Building Massively Valuable Companies*. He is an Aspen Institute Crown fellow, a Marshall scholar at Oxford, and a graduate of Stanford University.

Amir Husain is the founder and CEO of the artificial intelligence company SparkCognition, a position he has held since 2013. In November 2018, he became founding CEO of SkyGrid, a Boeing and SparkCognition joint venture that is building an aerial operating system to power the next century of aviation. Husain is a serial entrepreneur, technologist, and author based in Austin, Texas. He has been named Austin's Top Technology Entrepreneur of the Year by EY, was listed as an Onalytica Top 100 Artificial Intelligence Influencer, and received the Austin Under 40 Technology and Science Award, among other accolades. Husain serves on the board of advisors for the computer science department at the University of Texas, Austin, and is a member of the Center for a New American Security Task Force on Artificial Intelligence and National Security. Husain has been awarded twenty-seven U.S. patents and has several pending applications. His work has been featured in outlets such as *Foreign Policy*, Fox Business News, and the U.S. Naval Institute's *Proceedings*. He is the author of the best-selling book *The Sentient Machine: The Coming Age of Artificial Intelligence* and a coauthor of *Hyperwar: Conflict and Competition in the AI Century*.

Nicole Y. Lamb-Hale is a managing director in the business intelligence and investigations practice of Kroll, a division of Duff & Phelps. Lamb-Hale is based in the Washington, DC, office, where her areas of focus include investigative due diligence in mergers and acquisitions transactions, regulatory compliance matters, and market entry support. Representative matters include regulatory due diligence and consulting in the context of national security, including matters related to the Committee on Foreign Investment in the United States, export controls, and sanctions; and global investigative due diligence on potential investors, joint venture partners, and supply chain partners. Lamb-Hale joined Kroll from Albright Stonebridge Group, where she was senior vice president. Previously, she served as an assistant secretary of commerce in the International Trade Administration at the U.S. Department of Commerce. As the department's principal on CFIUS, Lamb-Hale represented the department's interests in some of the most significant matters before CFIUS in recent history. Lamb-Hale leverages her understanding of the nuances of CFIUS and other U.S. government national security regulatory regimes for the benefit of her clients. She earned her AB from the University of Michigan and her JD from Harvard Law School.

Eric S. Lander is president and founding director of the Broad Institute of Massachusetts Institute of Technology (MIT) and Harvard University. A geneticist, molecular biologist, and mathematician, he is a professor of biology at MIT and a professor of systems biology at Harvard Medical School. From 2009 to 2017, Lander served as co-chair of the President's Council of Advisors on Science and Technology. He has played a pioneering role in the reading, understanding, and biomedical application of the human genome and was a principal leader of the Human Genome Project. His honors include the MacArthur Fellowship, Gairdner Foundation Award, Dan David Prize, and Breakthrough Prize in Life Sciences.

James Manyika is a senior partner at McKinsey & Company and chairman of the McKinsey Global Institute (MGI). At MGI he has led research and published on the digital economy, AI, future of work, and growth and productivity. Manyika has previously served as vice chair of the Global Development Council at the White House, on the U.S. Commerce Department's Digital Economy Board, and on the National Innovation Advisory Board. He also serves on the board of the Broad Institute. He is a distinguished fellow of the Stanford Institute for Human-Centered Artificial Intelligence and a fellow at DeepMind and the American Academy of Arts and Sciences. He was a nonresident senior fellow in economic studies at the Brookings Institution, a member of the Programming Research Group and the Robotics Research Lab at Oxford University, a fellow of Balliol College, a visiting scientist at NASA Jet Propulsion Labs, and a faculty exchange fellow at MIT. A Rhodes scholar, Manyika received his BSc in electrical engineering from the University of Zimbabwe as an Anglo-American scholar and his DPhil, MSc, and MA from Oxford University in robotics, mathematics, and computer science.

William H. McRaven is a professor of national security at the University of Texas, Austin's Lyndon B. Johnson School of Public Affairs, a retired U.S. Navy four-star admiral, and the former chancellor of the University of Texas (UT) system. He is also a leadership consultant, and maintains writing, speaking, and board commitments. During his time in the military, McRaven commanded special operations forces at every level, eventually taking charge of the U.S. Special Operations Command. As chancellor of the UT system, he led one of the nation's largest and most respected systems of higher education. McRaven is a national authority on U.S. foreign policy and has advised Presidents George W. Bush and Barack Obama and other U.S. leaders on defense issues. In 2018, he received the Judge William H. Webster Distinguished Service Award for a lifetime of service to his nation. In 2016, McRaven was named the recipient of the Ambassador Richard M. Helms Award by the CIA Officers' Memorial Foundation, and in 2015 he received the Intrepid Freedom Award for his distinguished service in defending the values of democracy. McRaven graduated from the University of Texas, Austin, with a degree in journalism and received his master's degree from the Naval Postgraduate School in Monterey.

Mira Patel is the lead for economic opportunity, including blockchain policy outreach, at Facebook. She previously served in the Obama administration, where she built multimillion-dollar partnerships and advised cabinet officials, including Secretary of State Hillary Rodham Clinton, on foreign affairs and economic policy. Patel serves on the Council on Foreign Relations' Term Member Advisory Board. She was formerly a Chan Zuckerberg Initiative fellow, Atlantic Council millennium fellow, and Point Foundation scholar. She holds a BA from Wellesley College and an MBA from the University of Pennsylvania's Wharton School.

DJ Patil is the head of technology at Devoted Health, a senior fellow at the Harvard Kennedy School's Belfer Center for Science and International Affairs, and an advisor to Venrock Partners. Patil was appointed by President Obama to be the first U.S. chief data scientist, where he established new health-care programs and criminal justice reforms and led national data efforts. He led the product teams at

RelateIQ and was a founding board member for Crisis Text Line. He previously served as chief scientist, chief security officer, and head of the analytics and data product teams at LinkedIn, and has also worked at Skype, PayPal, and eBay. As a member of the faculty at the University of Maryland, Patil helped start a major research initiative on numerical weather prediction. He has served as an American Association for the Advancement of Science science and technology policy fellow for the Department of Defense, co-chaired a major review of U.S. efforts to prevent bioweapons proliferation in Central Asia, and cofounded the Iraqi Virtual Science Library. In 2014 he was named a young global leader by the World Economic Forum. He has been awarded the Department of Defense Medal for Distinguished Public Service by Secretary of Defense Ash Carter for his national security efforts.

L. Rafael Reif is the seventeenth president of MIT, where he has fostered the growth of MIT's nonprofit online platform, edX, and helped MIT pioneer the role that online learning and credentials will play in the future of higher education. He created the MIT Innovation Initiative; established the Environmental Solutions Initiative, Abdul Latif Jameel World Education Laboratory, Abdul Latif Jameel World Water and Food Security Lab, and Abdul Latif Jameel Clinic for Machine Learning in Health; issued the MIT Plan for Action on Climate Change; and launched the Engine, a specialized "tough tech" accelerator. Reif's other major priorities include the Kendall Square Initiative, an ambitious redevelopment plan powered by MIT; the MIT-IBM Watson AI Lab; the MIT Quest for Intelligence; the Task Force on the Work of the Future; and the MIT Stephen A. Schwarzman College of Computing, the most significant reshaping of the institute since the 1950s. Last summer, Reif wrote an op-ed in the *New York Times* about U.S. technology leadership and the emergence of China. He has been a member of the MIT faculty since 1980.

Eric Schmidt is technical advisor to Alphabet, where he advises its leaders on technology, business, and policy issues. Schmidt joined Google in 2001 and helped grow the company from a Silicon Valley start-up to a global leader in technology. He served as Google's chief executive officer from 2001 to 2011 and executive chairman from 2011 to 2018, alongside founders Sergey Brin and Larry Page. Under his leadership, Google dramatically scaled its infrastructure and diversified its product offerings while maintaining a culture of innovation. Schmidt serves on the boards of the Mayo Clinic and Broad Institute, among others. His philanthropic efforts through the Schmidt Family Foundation focus on climate change, including support of ocean and marine life studies at sea, and education, specifically research and technology in the natural sciences and engineering. He is the founder of Schmidt Futures, a venture facility that helps people do more for others by applying science and technology thoughtfully and working together across fields. He is the coauthor of *The New Digital Age: Transforming Nations, Businesses, and Our Lives; How Google Works;* and *Trillion Dollar Coach: The Leadership Playbook of Silicon Valley's Bill Campbell.*

Adam Segal is the Ira A. Lipman chair in emerging technologies and national security and director of the Digital and Cyberspace Policy program at CFR. Previously, Segal was an arms control analyst for the China Project at the Union of Concerned Scientists. He has been a visiting scholar at Stanford University's Hoover Institution, MIT's Center for International Studies, the Shanghai Academy of Social Sciences, and Tsinghua University in Beijing. He has taught at Vassar College and Columbia University. He is the author of *The Hacked World Order: How Nations Fight, Trade, Maneuver, and Manipulate in the Digital Age*, which describes the increasingly contentious geopolitics of cyberspace; *Advantage: How American Innovation Can Overcome the Asian Challenge*; and *Digital Dragon: High-Technology Enterprises in China*. His work has appeared in the *Economist, Financial Times, Foreign Affairs, Foreign Policy,* and *Wall Street Journal*, among others, and he has written articles and book chapters on Chinese technology policy. Segal has a BA and PhD in government from Cornell University and an MA in international relations from Tufts University's Fletcher School of Law and Diplomacy.

Raj M. Shah is the cofounder and chairman of Arceo.ai, a cybersecurity start-up. He is also a visiting fellow at Stanford's Hoover Institution. Previously, he was the managing partner of the Pentagon's Defense Innovation Unit Experimental (DIUx), reporting to the secretary of defense. Shah led DIUx in its efforts to strengthen U.S. armed forces through contractual and cultural bridges between Silicon Valley and the Pentagon. Before that, Shah was senior director of strategy at Palo Alto Networks, which acquired Morta Security, where he had been chief executive officer and cofounder. He began his business career as a consultant with McKinsey & Company. Shah serves as an F-16 pilot in the Air National Guard and has completed multiple combat deployments. He holds an AB from Princeton University and an MBA from the University of Pennsylvania's Wharton School.

Laura D'Andrea Tyson is a distinguished professor of the Graduate School and faculty director of the Institute for Business and Social Impact at the Haas School of Business at the University of California (UC), Berkeley. She chairs the board of trustees of UC Berkeley's Blum Center for Developing Economies. From July to December 2018, she served as interim dean of the Haas School. Previously, she was the dean of the London Business School from 2002 to 2006 and of the Haas School from 1998 to 2001. Tyson was a member of the U.S. Department of State's Foreign Affairs Policy Board, as well as the Council on Jobs and Competitiveness and President's Economic Recovery Advisory Board, both under President Obama. She served in the Bill Clinton administration as the director of the National Economic Council from 1995 to 1996 and as chair of the Council of Economic Advisers from 1993 to 1995. She is a member of the boards of directors of AT&T, CBRE Group, Lexmark International, and Apex Swiss Holdings. Tyson is the coauthor of *Leave No One Behind*, a report for the United Nation's High-Level Panel on Women's Economic Empowerment.

Jerry Yang is the founding partner of the innovation investment firm AME Cloud Ventures, through which he works with and invests in technology entrepreneurs. He cofounded Yahoo! in 1995 and served on the board of directors until 2012. While at Yahoo he led several initiatives, including two of the biggest investments in the internet sector: Yahoo Japan and Alibaba. Yang serves as a director on the boards of Workday, Lenovo, and Alibaba. He also serves on a number of his portfolio boards, including Docker and DiDi; on Stanford University's board of trustees; and on the boards or advisory councils of the National Committee on U.S.-China Relations, Brookings China Center, and Committee of 100. Yang holds BS and MS degrees in electrical engineering from Stanford University. He is widely recognized as a visionary and pioneer in the internet technology sector.

TASK FORCE OBSERVERS

Observers participate in Task Force discussions but are not asked to join the consensus. They participate in their individual, not their institutional, capacities.

Amy Myers Jaffe is the David M. Rubenstein senior fellow for energy and the environment and director of the program on Energy Security and Climate Change at CFR. An expert on global energy policy, geopolitical risk, and energy and sustainability, Jaffe previously served as executive director for energy and sustainability at the University of California, Davis, and senior advisor for energy and sustainability in the office of the chief investment officer of the University of California's board of regents. Before joining UC Davis, Jaffe served as founding director of the Energy Forum at Rice University's Baker Institute for Public Policy. She has taught energy policy, business, and sustainability courses at Rice University, UC Davis, and Yale University. Jaffe is widely published, including as coauthor of *Oil, Dollars, Debt and Crises: The Global Curse of Black Gold* with Mahmoud El-Gamal and coeditor of *Natural Gas and Geopolitics From 1970 to 2040*. She is chair of the steering committee of the Women in Energy Initiative at Columbia University's Center for Global Energy Policy. Jaffe was awarded the Senior Fellow Award from the U.S. Association for Energy Economics in 2015 for her career contributions.

Gayle Tzemach Lemmon is an adjunct senior fellow at CFR and partner and chief marketing officer at Shield AI, a technology firm specializing in AI for national defense. She is the author of the *New York Times* best sellers *Ashley's War: The Untold Story of a Team of Women Soldiers on the Special Ops Battlefield* and *The Dressmaker of*

Khair Khana, about an entrepreneur who supported her community under the Taliban. *Ashley's War* is currently being developed into a film. Lemmon's next book, set in northeastern Syria, is slated for publication in 2020. Lemmon began writing about economic stability in conflict and postconflict zones after a decade covering politics at the ABC News Political Unit. She also led public policy analysis for the global investment firm PIMCO during the 2008 financial crisis. Her work from Afghanistan, Liberia, Rwanda, Syria, and beyond has appeared in the *Atlantic, Foreign Affairs*, and *Harvard Business Review*, among others. A board member of Mercy Corps and a member of the Bretton Woods Committee, Lemmon speaks Spanish, German, and French and is conversant in Dari and Kurmanji. She holds an MBA from Harvard Business School.

Stewart M. Patrick is the James H. Binger senior fellow in global governance and director of the International Institutions and Global Governance program at CFR. From 2005 to 2008, he was a research fellow at the Center for Global Development, where he directed research and policymaking at the intersection of security and development. Patrick has also served on the U.S. State Department's policy planning staff, with lead staff responsibility for U.S. policy toward Afghanistan and a range of global and transnational issues. Before his government service, Patrick was a research associate at the Center on International Cooperation at New York University (NYU). He has taught at Johns Hopkins University's School of Advanced International Studies and NYU. Patrick is the author of *The Sovereignty Wars: Reconciling America With the World*. He has also written, cowritten, or edited five other books, including *Weak Links: Fragile States, Global Threats, and International*

Security. Additionally, Patrick writes the *Internationalist* blog for CFR. He graduated from Stanford University and received two MA degrees and a PhD in international relations from Oxford University, where he was a Rhodes scholar.

Anya Schmemann (ex officio) is Washington director of global communications and outreach and director of the Independent Task Force Program at CFR. She recently served as assistant dean for communications and outreach at American University's School of International Service. At CFR, Schmemann has overseen over fourteen high-level Task Forces on a range of topics, including the future of work, Arctic strategy, nuclear weapons, climate change, immigration, trade policy, and internet governance, and on U.S. policy toward Afghanistan, Brazil, North Korea, Pakistan, and Turkey. Schmemann previously managed communications at the Harvard Kennedy School's Belfer Center for Science and International Affairs and administered the Caspian Studies program there. She coordinated a research project on Russian security issues at the EastWest Institute and was assistant director of CFR's Center for Preventive Action, focusing on the Balkans and Central Asia. Schmemann received a BA in government and an MA in Russian studies, both from Harvard University, and she was a Truman national security fellow.

Contributing CFR Staff

Maria Teresa Alzuru
Senior Product Manager,
Product and Design

Sabine Baumgartner
Photo Editor, Product and Design

Patricia Lee Dorff
Editorial Director, Publishing

Lauren Dudley
Research Associate, Asia Studies

Julie Hersh
Production Editor, Publishing

Lorand Laskai
Research Associate, Digital and
Cyberspace Policy Program

Cayla Merrill
Associate Design Director,
Product and Design

Will Merrow
Data Visualization Designer,
Product and Design

Anya Schmemann
Director, Independent Task
Force Program

Chelie Setzer
Assistant Director, Independent
Task Force Program

Sara Shah
Program Associate, Washington
Meetings and Independent Task
Force Program

Kanzanira Thorington
Research Associate, Digital and
Cyberspace Policy Program

Katherine Vidal
Deputy Design Director,
Product and Design

Contributing Volunteer Interns

Artur Barkan
Volunteer Intern,
Independent Task Force Program

Caroline Fernandez
Volunteer Intern, Publishing

Aena Khan
Volunteer Intern,
Independent Task Force Program

Joy London
Volunteer Intern,
Independent Task Force Program

Amanda Long
Volunteer Intern,
Independent Task Force Program